D1709673

Dan Barasch

Ruin and Redemption in Architecture

12
Lost

64
Reimagined

Foreword   Dylan Thuras

My first love was with a flourmill on the banks of the Mississippi River in Minneapolis, Minnesota. It was part of the Washburn "A" Mill, owned by the Washburn-Crosby Company, but everyone called it Gold Medal Flour after the three-story red neon sign crowning the building. This gargantuan structure of towering grain silos and rusting metal skyways suspended in the air offered nine stories of adventure. At fifteen, I couldn't get enough of it.

Once the largest flour mill in the world, in the late 1800s it made enough flour in a single day for 12 million loaves of bread. This behemoth, and other gigantic mills nearby, once defined Minneapolis, giving rise to the city's nickname Mill City. But as flour milling dwindled, replaced with new economies in advertising and the arts, the mill shut in 1965. In 1991 the building suffered a massive fire. It was an enormous and notorious ruin, a holdover from a Minneapolis that no longer existed. My summer romance with this cathedral of concrete didn't begin until the late 1990s, and though its neon sign had been dark for over three decades, it was a beacon too bright to ignore.

Summer nights between my sophomore and junior years of high school were spent sneaking into Gold Medal Flour and exploring. In the winter, the mill's iron-rung ladders were freezing cold even through gloved hands. The ruins had to be traversed carefully. Huge holes where milling machinery had once been went eight stories deep. The building was vast, and the secrets its unfolding space revealed kept me returning.

In 1998, on the Fourth of July, friends and I climbed into the building, up the concrete stairs, and emerged on the rooftop – surprised to find it full of other people. Some were our age, just teenagers, but others were in their thirties or forties. This mix of graffiti kids, photographers, even a local professor, were all in thrall of the building. Climbing to the top of the old water tower provided the best view of downtown Minneapolis I've ever seen, and that night everyone knew they weren't going to find a better spot in Minneapolis. Together we drank cheap beer, told stories of rumored subterranean passages, and watched fireworks explode over the Mississippi River.

Emotional relationships with architecture, with places, are for me an unavoidable aspect of human existence. Nowhere is this personal interaction with architecture more interesting than in places where a building (or tunnel, or railway, or town) has ceased to serve its intended purpose. They occupy a shadowy liminal space between self-destruction and the possibility of rebirth.

Why are people are drawn to abandoned spaces? The late-eighteenth-century Romantics were certainly enamored with ruins. They saw in them a kind of architectural mortality, a *memento mori* for civilization. But as much as the Romantics' meditation on mortality is a piece of the draw, there's another axis to the attraction: the pull of the architect.

For me exploring abandoned buildings isn't about reveling in their collapse at all. The architecture of these buildings is present and potent, made more so by the lack of people and purpose. With their uncertain existence,

these spaces thrum with potential. An art gallery? A party space? Though my teenage mind couldn't quite stretch this far, off in the hazy distance were bigger ideas: reintegration into the city, reinterpretation and re-use. It's not the ruins themselves, but the unscripted architecture that produces the frisson.

As a teenager I was desperate to interact with the mill, to help bring it to life in some way. Inside it was alive, one of the most active graffiti locations in the city. Uninterrupted by the public and for the most part the police, it was where graffiti artists went to paint elaborate murals and try out new styles. I spent countless days there, exploring, painting, or just reading on the rooftop. Architecture and ruin purists tend to hate graffiti, believing that it detracts from the space itself, but say what you will, the artists who spent days painting in Gold Medal Flour were in active conversation with the building. It was graffiti that first taught me how to read the build environment, to see the city as layers of possibility, the hidden narratives of its alleyways, rooftops, and industrial spaces. It brought me to parts of the city I would never have otherwise explored and gave every street a personality.

I left Minneapolis in 2000 and began the odd life path that eventually led to the co-creation of Atlas Obscura, which is at its heart a celebration of space and place. The Atlas database of unusual and wondrous places includes many abandoned spaces, but also spaces of creative re-use. It is an eclectic mix of outsider art, catacombs, and strange museums; locations that fill your mind with possibility.

Not long after I left Minneapolis, Gold Medal Flour started its own transformation. The neon sign was switched on shortly after I left, and by the mid-2000s half of the building was converted into luxury apartments. Alongside, one of the most ruinous parts was converted into the Mill City Museum which tells the story of early Minneapolis and its mill workers. Its ninth floor observation deck offers almost the same vantage point as mine on that memorable Fourth of July.

Curiously, the other half of the mill building has never been converted and remains a ruin. Nearly twenty years later, the ruins and the museum call to me equally; past and future in one great structure. I'm overjoyed to see the potential of the space beautifully realized, and forever in love with the limitless possibility found in ruins.

Introduction   **Ruin and Redemption**
                                in Architecture
                                Dan Barasch

A fourth-generation New Yorker, I have devoted the last decade to the idea of transforming an abandoned underground trolley-car terminal in New York into a vibrant, new, public green space. This experience has led me on a fascinating journey, in the course of which I have met many people like me—neither designers nor architects, but simply those who are intrigued and inspired by abandoned spaces. It has also made me question why we are often so passionate about saving, reimagining, and transforming these types of structures.

When visiting my grandmother in New York's Lower East Side neighborhood in the 1980s, I would fixate on the decayed allure of tenement buildings near her apartment. Clustered like forlorn, desiccated soldiers, these were the survivors of a battle against mid-century urban decay. I was somewhat startled, and even a little afraid, when walking past them—their windows boarded up with plywood, their flashes of hieroglyphic graffiti, and chipped paint from rusty fire escapes on the sidewalks below. My parents warned me not to go any closer. But I would stare at those buildings and imagine my own great-grandparents, who had moved into similar tenement blocks immediately after their arrival at Ellis Island in the early twentieth century, living and eating, and falling in love, inside buildings that were abandoned decades later. I wondered about the last inhabitant to live in any of them. I wondered what they looked like inside, if anyone had left behind a fading photograph or a toothbrush or a broken mirror. I longed to explore the rubble behind the bright-yellow "Caution" tape.

In my mid-twenties, I moved into a neighborhood in Williamsburg, Brooklyn, at a time when the area's industrial sites and brownfield lots remained largely vacant, with derelict factory buildings hugging the East River waterfront. I would weave in and around the lonely sites by bicycle, allowing myself to take in the full effect of these forgotten, rusting hulks of metal and brick. It was a predominantly industrial district, without residential buildings, which lent a quiet, spooky feeling to the streets. Local artists and musicians would host parties inside some of these neglected warehouses. In an era before the smartphone, to reach a party you'd follow the pulsing sounds of loud—not necessarily great—rock bands or electronic beats that led to an unmarked building. Inside, hundreds or even thousands of revelers danced and drank cans of beer, sharing the secret of a cool-kid party. These places were almost certainly not legal entertainment venues; that was the whole point. We needed to creatively repurpose a site, where we maybe shouldn't have been, in order to feel free and inspired in a big city that could otherwise swallow you up and make you feel small and jaded. Reclaiming buildings as our own, making them new, making them real—making them *ours*—we brought them to pounding, blinding, stunning life . . . if only for a handful of hours before dawn reclaimed the city's silver-steel and piercing-glass skyline. At that point, I hadn't yet fully grasped the reality of gentrification, or my inadvertent role in it. I just knew that these abandoned buildings could offer a magical escape.

On a recent hike in the woods with my partner and young son, we came across a crumbling old warehouse foundation, long ago abandoned, with spidery green vines and armies of weeds almost entirely engulfing a sagging, roofless, brick structure. It had been disused for so long that nature had all but fully reclaimed it: some trees had boldly taken root amid chunks of rocky concrete and splintery wood panels. The only traces of human interaction were graffiti tags across the remaining "bones" of the buildings and etchings left by young couples or wanderers—those seeking immortality by making it clear that *they had been there*, communicating with future visitors with open-faced defiance in bright, unavoidable color. No one was around to explain what this space had once been. I felt a familiar twinge of excitement mixed with danger. We stared at the ruins for a few moments, daydreamed silently about what that site might once have been, and carried on.

Abandoned buildings are, in the most literal sense, mere shells of what they once were. They are exoskeletons—bruised and battered clues to the full story of their rise and fall. They often force us to rely on our curiosity and imagination for context. It is up to us to discover the narrative of a deserted building's past, and up to us to imagine—or even determine—its future. When we visit such places, we can imagine not merely what the space might have been but also what it could become. Abandoned spaces are of more profound significance to us than we may realize.

Once they are abandoned, the fates of spaces or structures will follow one of four possible directions—each of which is explored in this book. First, abandoned buildings may be destroyed or demolished, despite inspiring deep fascination or holding significant architectural or cultural relevance. An opening chapter focuses on these "lost" spaces, which offer cautionary tales to preservationists in recalling the grandeur of New York's Penn Station or Paris's Les Halles—or even well-intentioned public-housing icons like St. Louis's Pruitt-Igoe or East London's Robin Hood Gardens—all of which were demolished in the name of now debatable definitions of social and economic progress. A second chapter looks at "forgotten" abandoned sites—from empty World War II sea forts to Olympic Villages—that lack any significant schemes to reinvigorate them, and which remain haunted, vulnerable shells. "Reimagined" sites are explored in a third chapter, offering an optimistic if uncertain view of transformation proposals, with a particular focus on a growing worldwide trend: the reclamation of abandoned urban infrastructure for the creation of new public parks. And a fourth chapter observes a set of dramatically "transformed" structures—from abandoned train trestles to grain silos, and from churches to factories—all of which represent significant architectural achievements. The full scope of original and anticipated roles for these sites will be explored—from the highly commercial, to the whimsical, to the community-oriented—as well as projects that are both the result of bottom-up activism and those that were made possible by top-down, private investment or political will. These four chapters aim to collectively chart the unexpected journeys of abandoned spaces, and to better understand the larger story of what inspires their preservation, reimagination, and transformation—or the factors leading to their demolition or neglect.

My love for New York, and my interest in imagining new uses for underutilized spaces, first led me to imagine a new future for that most democratic of urban terrains: the New York underground. In this bewildering, chaotic subway system, every walk of life stands or sits side by side, hurtling in subway cars through dark tunnels and shuffling through poorly lit, poorly ventilated platforms, before reemerging above ground at a given destination. The urban underground is the lifeblood, the circulatory system, and perhaps the very soul of the city itself. Judged unsanitary and unsafe in the 1970s and 1980s, and regarded as a symbol of urban decay, the New York City Subway now feels relatively safe, sanitized, utilitarian, and sterile—at least to longtime New Yorkers.

I initially pursued the idea of creating an organization dedicated to producing irreverent, imaginative, roving art installations throughout the subway system, using that democratic space to inspire and offer free beauty, moving beyond its quotidian purpose as a means of getting from point A to B. Busy and preoccupied as they are, I thought that New Yorkers deserved and should even expect a bit of beauty in their underground tunnels. In one of the most creative cities on the planet, this seemed a way in which to use the specific constraints and opportunities of the subway system to change the way that art is conceived, made, and experienced. I imagined that it might have even changed the way in which people thought about the underground. But I abandoned this effort initially, choosing to focus on other jobs and projects.

A year or two later, a close friend, James Ramsey, suggested that I get involved with the Lowline. When I learned of his plan to transform an abandoned former trolley-car terminal on the Lower East Side into a new green space and public park, it felt like a perfect mix of my passions for the New York underground and for abandoned spaces in general. James had recently learned of this site at the heart of the Lower East Side neighborhood, near my family's stomping grounds and a few blocks from the office of his design firm, Raad Studio. The empty space was fascinating: a football field in size, built in 1908 but abandoned in 1948, complete with original Belgian blocks, U-shaped rail lines, catenary tracks, and even an abandoned control station tower that felt like a haunted house. On our first tour of the underground site, I remember feeling chills; we mused that the station tower could become a brilliant tree house for children. Situated squarely below a major bridge connecting Williamsburg to Manhattan, the former terminal felt like a magical discovery, right in the middle of a heavily congested and historically dense neighborhood. City and State officials, who operate and retain access to the site, were unaware of its history or even its existence—and nearly all community members, who had lived in and around the forgotten station all their lives, were also surprised to learn of the historic gem hidden below their sidewalks.

Partnering with James and a growing team of enthusiastic volunteers, we set up a nonprofit social enterprise organization to further develop the concept. James's design team developed architectural renderings of the proposed subterranean-park concept, in which new optical technology delivered natural daylight underground, filling the space with brilliant lighting alongside whimsical plants and meandering pathways. Armed with our enthusiasm for the idea, a promising technology concept, evocative renderings—and the recent example of Manhattan's own elevated park, the High Line—we set about talking to anyone who would listen to us about the possibility of bringing this idea to reality. We built a prototype exhibit of the underground-park concept in an abandoned former market building. We gathered support from all local officials representing the neighborhood. We hosted dozens of community events and workshops to engage local residents in the development of the idea, and raised several million dollars from private supporters. We then focused on building the Lowline Lab, a long-term technology-testing space and free exhibition venue, which allowed us to pilot the idea in all four seasons. In 2016 the City of New York provided an official endorsement for the concept, and efforts began for the formation of a capital campaign to build the underground park.

Even with all this momentum, however, the Lowline faces enormous challenges. Remediating a hundred-year-old subterranean ruin isn't cheap, and it is certainly not easy to execute a design scheme including innovative applications of solar technology and landscape design in a dense urban ecosystem. The project also faces a "labyrinth" of legal, technical, and political issues, any of which could potentially stall or even doom the effort.

But regardless of the fate of the Lowline project, I have gained an extraordinary glimpse into a world of design concepts related to abandoned sites. I have had the privilege of getting to know a wide range of individuals—some architects, but many not—who have dedicated significant amounts of their lifetimes to the redevelopment of abandoned spaces. In cities and towns across the United States and around the world, I met people dreaming of radically transforming abandoned spaces in very exciting ways. These projects sometimes never got off the ground, and sometimes were unable to protect buildings from demolition. But many have made, and are making, tremendous progress toward executing a transformation scheme. And sometimes, these schemes succeed. The more I spoke with others seeking to transform abandoned spaces with new concepts, the more fascinated I became by the question of what exactly attracts people to such spaces. Every one of these transformation projects stemmed from a deep and profound connection with the abandoned site, either because of its architectural merit, its former use or purpose, its raw state of decay, or its strategic and compelling location.

Ruin and Redemption in Architecture therefore aims to summon up the magic and allure of abandoned spaces—to try to capture the essence of that undeniable excitement and sense of adventure that we might feel when encountering an architectural ruin. But I think there is more to take away from this subject than just pretty pictures of old crumbling buildings, or even of inspiring new designs.

Many books have explored this phenomenon from two different angles—through categories that are usually described as "ruin porn" or "design porn." The former primarily showcases the extraordinary beauty of forgotten spaces, capturing moody photographs of wild weeds in unexpected places, neon-bright graffiti, or crumbling concrete—and the viewer cannot help but feel a sense of melancholy and adventure. Imagery in the latter category presents fascinating architectural renderings or finished structures that successfully repurpose disused spaces.

While ruin porn tends to offer sumptuous photographic collections it also regularly leaves the reader unable to make sense of the deeper meaning, or even the strong emotions, that these images might evoke. The proliferation of this type of imagery also reflects the urgency needed to capture or highlight abandoned spaces before they are permanently demolished. Meanwhile, design porn is often more visual or technical in nature, but it focuses on the genius of the architect or designer rather than on the latent potential of the site or building itself. This book seeks to move beyond both categories: it captures the energy and excitement of that most elemental human moment of discovery of abandoned spaces while also exploring the broader, societal implications that arise when working in this realm.

With the decline of the industrial era and the rise of a new digital age, there is a growing sense of change in all aspects of modern life. Our cities are becoming denser and more crowded, necessitating the reuse and reimagination of obsolete industrial buildings. Rising income inequality has led to heightened insecurity among vulnerable populations. Social life increasingly takes place online or on our phones; we often spend more time on social networks than in personal contact with friends and family. The growing impact of this suggests that we feel increasingly divided and isolated from each other. Opportunities to connect physically, in public or private, seem increasingly precious.

This may be why many of the proposed reinventions in *Ruin and Redemption* involve repurposing derelict spaces for artistic, cultural, or community purposes—reclaiming these structures for public use. The irony, however, is that efforts to repurpose such structures into new, popular community spaces can lead to an exacerbation of social inequality. Abandoned buildings tend to be in poorer or more neglected neighborhoods, since city planners or real estate developers had not previously found it desirable or profitable to invest in those districts. Attempts to transform them into new attractions, which in turn frequently lead to an increase in surrounding land values and further investment, may unwittingly ease the path for the "viral" effects of gentrification.

Amid these cultural and economic changes, abandoned structures themselves serve as proxies for old ways of life, or means of enterprise, that are no longer viable.

It is natural to feel nostalgic for these lost social functions, and the buildings that housed them. Many of us yearn for a connection to our shared history and a sense of authenticity—a physical connection between our uncertain future and our imagined past. It is as if we can feel the "wisdom" of older spaces, just as we are sometimes suspicious of newer designs.

Yet many inspired preservation or revitalization schemes are often unable to move ahead. Despite the most passionate efforts to save or reimagine an abandoned building, an innovative idea can be doomed by market forces, technical issues, or shifting political winds. These unsuccessful efforts serve as more than historical footnotes, however; they offer warnings and lessons to those of us who see the allure and potential of abandoned spaces. Some of the projects included in this book have, in fact, extremely uncertain futures—the Lowline is among them—and may fail to proceed, or may move in dramatically different and entirely unforeseen directions, in the years ahead.

Ultimately, when transforming abandoned buildings, we must also question the very concept of "success" and "failure." Even projects that successfully preserve or transform abandoned buildings represent a kind of loss. Time cannot be reversed, a space cannot be unabandoned, and the past can never be truly reclaimed. Once fallen into disuse, a structure will never be exactly as it was. Beautiful abandoned buildings can be transformed into far less inspiring structures than their original selves. The peaceful mystery of a deserted space may be transformed into the bustle of a frenetic thoroughfare. In an age of hyper-development, there are those who will maintain that abandoned sites were better off before these design interventions no matter how celebrated or popular they become. This survey suggests an emerging discussion about the positive and negative outcomes—intended and unintended—of proposals for abandoned sites.

Whether abandoned structures are ultimately lost, forgotten, reimagined, or transformed, they meant something to someone at some point in time, and their disuse represents a kind of tear in the social fabric. Attempts to repair these "wounds," no matter how well meaning or well executed, always leave scars.

The broader meaning of abandoned spaces transcends their beauty or even their ability to thrill, frighten, or inspire. They are more than shells for architects to revive with innovative designs. They are opportunities to play with history. We might try to destroy or demolish our history, preserve it in amber, or radically transform it into something bold and fresh. When taking stock of an abandoned building, we are given a chance to make things right, to fix the injustices of the past—if only on a single site, in a particular location. We are given the chance to redefine who decides what a space should and can be. And if the stars align, we might just reclaim it as our own.

1

Lost

Cyclorama Center
Gettysburg, PA, USA
Richard Neutra

Government Center
Goshen, NY, USA
Paul Rudolph

Les Halles
Paris, France
Victor Baltard

Sanzhi UFO Houses
New Taipei City, China
Hung Kuo Group

Pan Am Worldport
New York, NY, USA
Ives, Turano, and Gardner

Singer Building
New York, NY, USA
Ernest Flagg

Schiller Theater Building
Chicago, IL, USA
Adler and Sullivan

Hall of Nations
New Delhi, India
Raj Rewal

Larkin Administration
Buffalo, NY, USA
Frank Lloyd Wright

Trotting Park
Goodyear, AZ, USA
Ivonne Grassetto

Palace of the Republic
Berlin, Germany
Graffunder, Prasser et al

Imperial Hotel
Tokyo, Japan
Frank Lloyd Wright

West Pier
Brighton, England
Eugenius Birch

Château de Noisy
Houyet, Belgium
Edward Milner

Penn Station
New York, NY, USA
McKim, Mead and White

Prentice Women's Hospital
Chicago, IL, USA
Bertrand Goldberg

Birmingham Central Library
Birmingham, England
John Madin

Robin Hood Gardens
London, England
Alison and Peter Smithson

Pruitt-Igoe
St. Louis, MO, USA
Minoru Yamasaki

In the world of humanity, nothing lasts forever. The structures that we build, to shelter or transport or entertain us, also reflect a human cadence: the enthusiasm of youth, a period of productive efficiency, a slow or sudden decline. Once a building is no longer useful, we often find it hard to fully abandon. But sometimes we must both abandon and subsequently destroy a building. Over time, architectural marvels and eyesores alike are destroyed for any number of reasons: obsolescence, shifting political priorities, or some calculation of costs and benefits. Along the path to destruction, some receive significant attention, as beloved or iconic structures that inspire efforts of preservation or reimagining. Whether the preservation battle is a fierce protest or an academic affair, there is always a sense of loss when a lofty design is reduced to a dusty pile of rubble.

Destroying architecture means reckoning with history, and reckoning with history is a tricky business. Once a physical building is demolished, its past cannot be replicated, but nostalgia for its former glory often lives on. The baroque Berlin City Palace (Stadtschloss) in the eastern part of the German capital, formerly home to the Prussian royal family and dating to the fifteenth century, sustained significant damage during World War II. It was destroyed rather than preserved in 1950, despite widespread criticism, in an effort by the communist regime to downplay the Prussian military era. Built in its place was the socialism-inspired Palace of the Republic (Palast der Republik), which would house the East German Parliament between 1976 and 1990, along with large and popular venues for political meetings and cultural events. After the fall of the Berlin Wall, in September 1990, the *Volkskammer* (People's Chamber) voted to demolish the building, citing asbestos concerns but also to shed a visceral testament to the communist era. In an ironic twist, the German Bundestag (federal parliament) in 2003 agreed to demolish the Palast der Republik and rebuild a replica of the Stadtschloss. Becoming one of Europe's most expensive projects, at six hundred million Euros, the rebuilt palace was rebranded the Humboldt Forum. It seeks to underscore a deep understanding of German history and broader social inter-disciplinary programming, in exhibition spaces the size of three football fields. Poised for a new era, the Humboldt Forum will nonetheless attain neither the grandeur of the Stadtschloss nor the cool efficiency of the Palast.

The pain associated with the loss of inspiring architecture is doubled when the site becomes transformed into a place of minimal social value. Once one of the tallest build-ings in Chicago, the 1,300-seat Schiller Theater Building, constructed to house the German Opera Company, was considered among the most beautiful buildings in the city, beloved for its ornate proscenium arches. In the 1950s, after the theater's decline and during a broad sweep of urban-renewal efforts by the City of Chicago, the building was slated for demolition, kicking off an unsuccessful preservation battle. Destroyed in 1961, the site was transformed into a forlorn parking structure. Frank Lloyd Wright's first public commission, the stately red-brick Larkin Administration Building in Buffalo, was designed for the Larkin mail-order soap business and became broadly viewed as an architectural gem, with its 76-foot (23-meter), five-story-high central skylit courtyard; innovative design technologies; a giant Moehler Pipe Organ; and elegant, bespoke, built-in furniture. Destroyed in 1950 after the company was forced to sell the building, the site was also transformed into a parking lot, featuring a lonely brick pier and commemorative plaque. Both of these buildings were destroyed before the modern preservationist movement gained momentum in the United States.

The heartbreaking destruction of the original Penn Station in New York served as a turning point in contempo-rary historic preservation. Built as the central rail hub for a rapidly expanding city, it opened in 1910 and ushered passengers into North America's most ambitious metropolis in stunning Classical style, featuring a coffered 148-foot (45-meter) ceiling and skylights drenching the atrium and platforms below with brilliant daylight, while covering 8 acres (3.2 hectares) in the center of Manhattan. But mounting losses by the railroad company, coupled with a lack of significant preservationist support for the Beaux-Arts structure, led to its demolition in 1963. In its place a bland, charmless Penn Station facility was built below a massive entertainment arena, Madison Square Garden. Despite its role as the largest transportation hub in the United States, serving over 650,000 commuters daily, it remains today a utilitarian maze of poorly lit tunnels, confused wayfind-ing, and low-ceilinged, claustrophobic passageways. The architectural historian Vincent Scully observed that in the original Penn Station, "one entered the city like a God," while with the new station, "one scuttles in now like a rat." Shock and dismay at the lost architectural gem led to the creation of the Landmarks Preservation Commission in New York, which would go on to save myriad sites of the city's architectural significance over the ensuing decades and usher in new generations of preservationist thinking in cities around the world.

Demolished architectural sites may be repurposed for similar functions, but are usually pale reflections of the originals. Frank Lloyd Wright's Imperial Hotel in Tokyo, built in 1923, would withstand major earthquakes and bombing during World War II, only to be destroyed in 1968 to make way for a more efficient and less lyrical high-rise hotel tower. The Singer Building in New York, an early forty-seven-story skyscraper completed in 1908 with a charming red-brick, stone, and terracotta exterior, was once the tallest building in the world. In 1968, after its owners moved uptown, it became the tallest building ever to be dismantled, only to be replaced with a relentlessly corporate black-glass tower. The Brutalist Orange County Government Center, designed by architect and dean of the Yale School of Architecture, Paul Rudolph, opened in 1967 and was both lauded as an inventive design for pro-gressive government and scorned as an inefficient eyesore. The unique structure, composed of three buildings with 87 roofs, was partially demolished in 2015, giving way to new structures that have been widely criticized for destroying the overall effect of the initial design if not the entire structure.

Few buildings carry more emotional power than those designed for public housing. Government-subsidized housing must consider a wide array of livability and sustainability questions for society's most vulnerable members. The Brutalist Robin Hood Gardens in London, designed by Alison and Peter Smithson, featured innovative design elements including "streets in the sky," internal elevated passageways, and alcoves to encourage social interaction. After a period of decline and despite considerable preservation attempts, the 252 apartments were demolished in 2017, with plans for a new 1,575-unit development and a museum to commemorate the original design. The Modernist Pruitt-Igoe complex in St. Louis, by World Trade Center designer Minoru Yamasaki, was built in 1954. Suffering from poorly considered maintenance issues, it quickly declined, leading to its demolition in 1970. In São Paulo, Brazil, the Edificio São Paulo, an abandoned tower that was claimed by over three thousand indigent residents as informal, vertical housing, was proposed as permanent public housing but was ultimately destroyed. The destruction, rather than reclaiming, of these formal and informal structures open larger questions of the potential of design to solve social issues, and challenges the very concept of public housing.

Some buildings are so beautiful or architecturally significant that demolitions are especially controversial. The Indian Hall of Nations, the largest exhibition center in New Delhi, inaugurated by Prime Minister Indira Gandhi in 1972 and designed by architect Raj Rewal, was the world's first and largest space-frame concrete structure, covering nearly 150 acres (607,000 square meters) and widely recognized as possessing significant architectural merit. The broadly unpopular destruction of the structure in 2017 was completed overnight, despite the protests of a variety of Indian and international organizations. The Jorba Laboratories building in Madrid, an iconic Modernist concrete structure designed by Spanish architect Miguel Fisac, featured a stack of five square floors offset at 45-degree angles with concrete panels unifying the exterior; it was destroyed in 1999. These and other losses have led to a growing dialog on the need to redefine noteworthy modern buildings as deserving of heritage protection.

Some mid-century, futuristic structures were so singular, so quirky, or so weird that their demolition was perceived as a significant loss. The brightly colored spaceship-shaped Sanzhi pods in Taiwan, China, built in 1978 to resemble the space age 1960s Futuro houses, were originally envisioned as a vacation resort for U.S. military officers. Labeled "UFO houses" for their unusual flying-saucer design, the site would never fully open after a series of bizarre accidents, mysterious suicides, and even a Dutch graveyard unearthed on the site's grounds. Incomplete in 1980 due to construction losses, and demolished in 2010, efforts then began to transform the land into a resort and water park. In 1962, Richard Neutra designed The Cyclorama for the U.S. Civil War site of Gettysburg, Pennsylvania, in the shape of a three-story cylinder to display a 360-degree painting of the pivotal 1863 battle.

Opening to great fanfare at the time, it was later dubbed a bizarre distraction from the integrity of the location's natural beauty. The U.S. National Park Service confirmed plans to destroy the structure before the battle's 150th anniversary, making way for a new museum and visitor center designed to resemble a nineteenth-century farm.

The Pan Am Worldport, built in 1960 at New York's John F. Kennedy Airport, was an instantly iconic symbol of the grand early era of aviation, with a terminal resembling a spaceship, featuring a 114-foot (35-meter) circular, cantilevered roof. After the demise of Pan American World Airlines in 1991, the airport was described as out of date and obsolete, and eventually was demolished in 2013. Some buildings are so quirky that it becomes difficult to imagine their future uses.

The same is true for extraordinarily beloved late-nineteenth-century structures, which seem too difficult to maintain in the twentieth century. The Château de Noisy in Belgium, built in 1866, was abandoned by its owners by 1991 after a steady decline and the difficulty of maintaining the old structure, and it was demolished in 2017. Les Halles, the traditional central market of Paris, was transformed in 1853 by Victor Baltard with elegant, iconic glass-and-iron buildings, but found itself unable to compete with modern markets and retail options in the mid-twentieth century. The structure and market were removed in 1971, transformed into a modern shopping mall and transit hub. The West Pier in Brighton in England, designed by Eugenius Birch, was a popular pier built to attract tourism to the coastal city in 1866. After a period of decline, it closed in 1975; suffered a series of collapses in 2002 and 2003; and was partly demolished in 2010. In its place, the British Airways i360 observation tower offers an entirely different, and further removed, view of the surrounding harbor than its predecessor.

We miss these lost buildings and structures, both for what they were and what they might have been in a modern era. Yet compelling buildings that are abandoned and then destroyed continue to offer us profound, powerful lessons from beyond the grave. It is only through their demolition that we appreciate the importance of defining our favorite spaces as worthy of historic preservation, and possible reimagining or repurposing. It is not merely the physical structures that we mourn but also the intention behind them, their ambition, their history, and their intended or unintended consequences. Buildings, be they grand or weird or beautiful or innovative, tell us about who we are and what we value, as a society and as a community. Our destructive impulses end up destroying more than steel and brick and stone. We destroy the irreplaceable magic of an inspiring space. In the short term, it may appear easier to destroy first and consider a rebuilding scheme later. But once we lose these buildings, we can never reclaim their energy, vitality, spirit, or beauty. As Joni Mitchell put it so well, we don't know what we've got until it's gone.

Cyclorama Center
Gettysburg, PA, USA
Richard Neutra
Completed 1962
Demolished 2013

△ The Cyclorama Center at the U.S. Civil War site of Gettysburg, Pennsylvania, was built in the shape of a three-story cylinder to display a 360-degree painting from 1883, featuring a pivotal battle of 1863, and the concrete modernist building opened to great fanfare.

▽ The quirky building was later dubbed a distraction from the integrity of the location's natural beauty. The U.S. National Park Service confirmed plans to destroy the structure before the battle's 150th anniversary, making way for a new museum and visitor center, resembling a nineteenth-century farm.

Government Center
Goshen, NY, USA
Paul Rudolph
Completed 1972
Demolished 2015

△ The Brutalist building, designed for local county officials north of New York City, was widely celebrated for its unique structure, composed of three buildings with eighty-seven roofs, and spaces laid out to maximize interaction among government officials.

▽ Criticized by some as an inefficient eyesore and partially demolished despite protests, a recent controversial addition has arguably destroyed the overall effect of the initial design, if not the entire structure.

Les Halles
Paris, France
Victor Baltard
Completed 1850
Demolished 1972

△ Les Halles, the traditional central market of Paris originally built in 1183, was transformed in 1850 into a fresh food market by Victor Baltard with elegant glass and iron buildings, becoming one of Paris's most iconic destinations.

▽ ▷ Unable to compete with modern markets and greater retail options available in the mid-twentieth century, the structure and market were removed, transformed into a modern shopping mall and transit hub.

Sanzhi UFO Houses
New Taipei City, China
Hung Kuo Group
Completed 1978
Demolished 2010

Δ   In Taipei City, a set of futuristic houses was built as a waterfront holiday resort, designed to attract U.S. military officers stationed in Asia and wealthy Taiwanese tourists. The uniquely designed and colorful "pods," shaped like UFOs, resembled and were inspired by "Futuro" housing by Matti Suuronen.

∇   Due to a series of failed investments, accidents on the site, and superstitious claims that the site was haunted, the buildings were not completed, and abandoned by 1980. The derelict site continued to be a popular spectacle for urban explorers, filmmakers and photographers until its demolition some thirty years later.

Pan Am Worldport
New York, NY, USA
Ives, Turano, and Gardner
Completed 1960
Demolished 2011

△ The Pan Am Worldport at New York's John F Kennedy Airport was an instantly iconic symbol of the grand early era of aviation, with a terminal resembling a spaceship, featuring a 114-foot (35-meter) circular cantilevered roof.

▽ After the demise of Pan American World Airlines in 1991, the airport was described as out of date and obsolete. It was eventually demolished two decades later, with the site reused for airport storage.

Singer Building
New York, NY, USA
Ernest Flagg
Completed 1908
Demolished 1968

△ Among the world's earliest skyscrapers and once the world's tallest office building, the forty-seven-story Beaux-Arts tower featured a red brick, stone, and terra cotta exterior and an opulent lobby—and was briefly considered a potential home for the New York Stock Exchange.

▽ In the late 1960s, the owners of the Singer Manufacturing Company moved its headquarters uptown, and the building became the tallest building ever to be intentionally demolished. It was replaced with a corporate tower of black glass.

Schiller Theater Building
Chicago, IL, USA
Adler and Sullivan
Completed 1892
Demolished 1961

△ Once one of the tallest buildings in Chicago, the 1,300-seat Schiller Theater Building, which was constructed to house the German Opera Company, was considered among the most beautiful buildings in the city, beloved for its ornate proscenium arches.

▽ In the 1950s, after the theater's decline and during a broad sweep of urban renewal efforts by the City of Chicago, the site was slated for demolition, kicking off an unsuccessful preservation battle. The building was razed, making way for a forlorn parking structure.

Hall of Nations
New Delhi, India
Raj Rewal
Completed 1972
Demolished 2017

△ Built as a global exhibition center to celebrate twenty-five years of Indian independence, the concrete space-frame pyramidal structure was the world's first and largest of its kind, and was considered a marvel of innovative design, engineering and architecture.

▽ ▷ Despite its significance, and its cultural importance for the postcolonial country, numerous preservation attempts were unable to stave off demolition. Only forty-five years after opening, it was destroyed as part of the India Trade Promotion Organisation's redevelopment plan.

Larkin Administration
Buffalo, NY, USA
Frank Lloyd Wright
Completed 1906
Demolished 1950

△ Wright's stately red brick building was designed for the Larkin mail-order soap business, and was regarded as an architectural gem, with its five-story-high central sky-lit courtyard, innovative design technologies, a giant Moehler Pipe Organ, and elegant bespoke built-in furniture.

▽ Destroyed in 1950 after the company was forced to sell the building, the site was transformed into a parking lot. The only remaining features of the former architectural icon are a lonely brick pier and commemorative plaque.

Trotting Park
Goodyear, AZ, USA
Ivonne Grassetto
Completed 1965
Demolished 2017

△ Built west of Phoenix, Arizona, in a remote desert location, the 194-acre (79-hectare) horseracing park was a large Futurist concrete structure with an imposing grandstand and sloping geometric balconies and passageways, costing nearly ten million dollars to build.

▽ The extremely hot climate of the outdoor park, in addition to the challenge of unpaved roads around it, led to its closure a year after opening. Abandoned for another fifty years, the site was used for occasional film shoots, remaining a site of curiosity until its demolition.

Palace of the Republic
Berlin, Germany
Graffunder, Prasser et al
Completed 1976
Demolished 2006

△ Built on the site of the former Berlin City Palace, the socialist-inspired Palace of the Republic became an East German landmark, housing both the parliament and large and popular cultural venues, including art galleries, a theater, a bowling alley, a post office, two auditoria, a discothèque and restaurants.

▽ After the fall of the Berlin Wall in 1990, the *Volkskammer* (People's Chamber) voted to demolish the building, citing asbestos concerns, but also to shed a visceral testament to the communist era. Ironically, officials agreed to rebuild a replica of the former palace on the site, rebranded as the Humboldt Forum.

Imperial Hotel
Tokyo, Japan
Frank Lloyd Wright
Completed 1923
Demolished 1968

△ This celebrated building in the Mayan Revival style was designed in the "H" shape of the hotel's own logo, updating an earlier version of the hotel, completed in 1880. The building served as inspiration for a set in the 2018 Wes Anderson film, *Isle of Dogs*.

∇ Due to structural damage from major earthquakes, damage during World War II, and a slow period of decay, the hotel was demolished and replaced with a new high-rise building. Portions of the building were saved and placed into the Museum Meiji-mura.

West Pier
Brighton, England
Eugenius Birch
Complete 1866
Partly Demolished 2010

△ The popular pier was designed to attract tourists to the coastal city, and offered a 1,000-foot (305-meter) promenade for swimmers. A concert hall and other entertainment venues were later added to the pier, and it became a major destination in the early twentieth century.

▽ After a period of decline following World War II, and due to high maintenance costs, the pier closed in 1975. It suffered a series of collapses in 2002 and 2003, and was partly demolished seven years later. A new observation tower offers an entirely different view of the surrounding harbor than its predecessor.

Château de Noisy
Houyet, Belgium
Edward Milner
Complete 1866
Demolished 2017

△ A Neo-Gothic palace designed in the Belgian countryside for French aristocrats fleeing the French Revolution, the Château Miranda was taken by a Belgian railway company during World War II. It was re-purposed into an orphanage, earning its nickname "Noisy Castle."

▽ The castle was abandoned in 1991 after steady decline, remaining in a state of disrepair and providing a site of fascination for ruin explorers. Due to the difficulty of maintaining the structure and a lack of interest in preservation, it was demolished more than two decades later.

Penn Station
New York, NY, USA
McKim, Mead and White
Complete 1910
Demolished 1963

△ The 8-acre (3.2-hectare) railroad station in midtown Manhattan was internationally recognized for its grand Beaux-Arts style, featuring coffered 148-foot (45-meter) ceilings and skylights that drenched the platforms with daylight.

∇ ▷ Mounting losses by the railroad company, coupled with a lack of significant preservationist support for the structure, led to its demolition. It was replaced with a bland, charmless facility built below the massive entertainment arena, Madison Square Garden.

3

TIME
DOWN STAIRS FOR
INCOMING
TRAINS
CHECK HERE
CHECK HERE
LONG ISLAND TRAINS

Prentice Women's Hospital
Chicago, IL, USA
Bertrand Goldberg
Completed 1975
Demolished 2014

△ This Brutalist concrete structure, with its unique nine-story quatrefoil shape sitting atop a five-story rectangular base, optimized the hospital's maternity unit by placing nurses at the core and patients in each of the four wings.

▽ Despite significant preservation attempts and redesign proposals, the building was decommissioned in 2011 and demolished several years later, making way for a new biomedical research center for its owner, Northwestern University.

Birmingham Central Library
Birmingham, England
John Madin
Completed 1974
Demolished 2015

△ Featuring a ziggurat style that was inspired by the libraries of ancient Mesopotamia, this Brutalist building was the largest non-national library in Europe upon opening, and for four decades it served as the primary library for the UK's second largest city.

▽ Following the city's decline from the 1970s onwards, the building was eventually slated for demolition. It was replaced by Paradise Circus, a redevelopment scheme for the neighborhood. All books and library materials were moved to the newly constructed Library of Birmingham.

Robin Hood Gardens
London, England
Alison and Peter Smithson
Completed 1972
Demolished 2017

△ The Brutalist Robin Hood Houses in London, designed by the Smithsons, featured innovative design elements including "streets in the sky," internal elevated passageways and alcoves that were intended to encourage social interaction and give shared amenity to residents.

▽ After a period of decline and despite considerable attempts at preservation, demolition of the 252 apartments began in 2017. A new 1,575-unit housing development is now partly complete on the site, and a museum is planned to commemorate the original design.

Pruitt-Igoe
St. Louis, MO, USA
Minoru Yamasaki
Completed 1954
Demolished 1970

△ A massive public housing complex, composed of 2,870 apartments on fifty-seven acres (twenty-three hectares) and designed to house ten thousand residents, the Pruitt-Igoe estate was built at the height of Modernism.

▽ Its large scale, modular construction logic was intended to provide housing efficiently but it quickly deteriorated, leading to the demolition of all thirty-three buildings in 1970. The project became an iconic symbol of the challenges of public housing.

Miami Marine Stadium
Miami, FL, USA
Hilario Candela

Power Plant IM
Charleroi, Belgium
State Architect

Buzludzha Monument
Kazanlak, Bulgaria
Georgi Stoilov

Olympic Stadium
Athens, Greece
Santiago Calatrava

Ryugyong Hotel
Pyongyang, North Korea
Baikdoosan Architects

PECO Delaware Station
Philadelphia, PA, USA
Windrim and Eglin

Michigan Central Station
Detroit, MI, USA
Reed and Stern

Glenwood Power Plant
Yonkers, NY, USA
Reed and Stern

Tempelhof Airport
Berlin, Germany
Ernst Sagebiel

Summer Olympic Village
Wustermark, Germany
State Architect

Gunkanjima Island
Japan
Mitsubishi Corporation

InTempo Building
Benidrom, Spain
Pérez-Guerras Arquitectos

Presidio Modelo
Nueva Gerona, Cuba
State Architect

Olympic Park
Sarajevo, Bosnia
Boreisa Bouchard

Lost

Flak Tower
Vienna, Austria
State Architect

Torre de David
Caracas, Venezuela
Enrique Gómez

Maunsell Sea Forts
Thames Estuary, England
Guy Maunsel l

Restaurante Panorâmico
Lisbon, Portugal
Chaves da Costa

Council of Ministries
Sukhumi, Georgia
State Architect

Forgotten

Spaces are abandoned all the time, for any number of reasons. New technologies may render a building irrelevant over time, with owners uninterested in any kind of conversion. Structures built during wartime, useful for defending cities from attacks, become eerie concrete ghosts after a conflict is over. Sometimes money runs out during construction; real estate developers may have no option but to cut their losses, abandon a project, and leave behind an incomplete exoskeleton of what could have been. Businesses go out of business. Entertainment venues fall out of favor or cannot attract sufficient audiences. Governments and public policies shift course, rendering public-funded architecture unviable. Sometimes it is easiest to simply and fully desert buildings or structures, leaving them to future generations to destroy or preserve.

This is not new, of course, but more a reflection of the human condition and the buildings we build. No piece of the built environment is ever destined to "live" forever, just as no physical structure can remain relevant and useful for all ages. And yet somehow the discovery of an obsolescent piece of architecture often elicits a profound sense of loss and nostalgia. The building need not be an architectural masterpiece, be particularly beautiful, or have been relatively beloved in its heyday. Some of the most bizarre or quotidian structures somehow generate enormous affection from contemporary visitors or residents, leading to preservation or protection efforts—perhaps with an eye toward reuse, perhaps not. Sometimes it is the mere fact of their abandonment, like a lonely orphan adrift, that draws our attention.

In recent decades, efforts by myriad international, domestic, and local institutions have led to the active preservation of a broad array of abandoned spaces. The inclusion of a site on UNESCO's World Heritage List offers an international stamp of approval of its cultural value for humanity, paving the way for a thoughtful future and creating a barrier to demolition. Nonprofit organizations such as the World Monuments Fund provide significant levels of visibility and advocacy for the preservation of sites otherwise at risk of destruction. Within individual countries, the addition of a building to a national heritage list or registry is often an important step toward preservation, and many regional or municipal governments also have similar mechanisms to safeguard forgotten architecture.

Elsewhere, benign or even abject neglect may allow a site to remain in place almost by accident, left to crumble around the edges, grow weeds between cracks, suffer the ravages of weather, and become a sprawling canvas for graffiti, vandalism, or illicit activity. For lovers of abandoned architecture, this is when the fun starts. Preserved, either by accident of history or by the forces of active intervention, these spaces can be described as "forgotten"—not officially slated for architectural redevelopment, or still in the very earliest stages of creative ideation. But this does not mean that these spaces have not already been repurposed, in one way or another. Before even the sketchiest of redesign concepts are imagined, many "forgotten" spaces become exciting destinations for the adventurous.

Urban explorers, forging a self-styled "urbex" community, actively seek out these kinds of spaces to visit, photograph, and seek a thrill that recalls childhood—the sense of wonder and delight that comes from being somewhere you're not supposed to be.

If the first unofficial use for these forgotten spaces is, then, a kind of irreverent tourism, the path of least resistance—and most immediate commercial use—is to use these sites for more official tourism. The Presidio Modelo in Cuba, a former prison that once housed a young Fidel Castro among scores of other political dissidents, has been a site of curiosity since its closure in 1966. Today, one can visit the unique panopticon-shaped structure with its guard tower at the center, blacked out to create a sense of omnipresent, omnidirectional surveillance. Hashima Island, off the coast of Japan near Nagasaki, was a prolific coal-mining facility operated by the Mitsubishi Corporation and powered by harsh forced labor from abroad. It was entirely abandoned by 1974. Inspired by the "ghost town" left untouched for decades, the site opened to tourists in 2009 and was added to the UNESCO World Heritage List in 2015. The dark, difficult, even horrific histories of both sites fade into historical footnotes as visitors are treated to a beautiful, unique, visceral experience of being transported back in time.

Shifting modes of transportation have led to various examples of forgotten architecture. As rail travel declined in the twentieth century—and Americans, in particular, grew more dependent on automobiles—some extraordinary rail-related architecture was left to rot within a variety of cities. The Buffalo Central Terminal, an impressive seventeen-story Art Deco building, served as the elegant rail midpoint between New York City and Chicago from 1929 to 1979. Despite multiple schemes to reclaim and reuse the building, the site remained forgotten for decades. In late 2017, the terminal was added to the World Monuments Watch List, with plans underway by the Central Terminal Restoration Corporation to preserve and restore the site. In Detroit, an enormous Beaux-Arts terminal, Michigan Central Station, was built in 1913 and carried passengers until 1988. Despite broad fascination with and affection for the building and its addition to the U.S. National Register of Historic Places, the structure remained under constant threat of demolition into the early twenty-first century. In an interesting twist of history, the Ford automobile company in 2018 announced plans to redevelop the property, in partnership with local government, as part of a broader local economic-development plan. These examples illustrate the desire to save stunning architectural buildings that have been cast aside, but also stem from a sense of regret and longing for forgotten ways of life. These train stations symbolize a lost era of American grandeur, recalling the romance of transportation hubs at a height of elegance and efficiency. The adventurous spirit of travel itself seems at stake in preserving and reusing these forgotten railway "fossils."

Another pattern that seems to emerge is the transformation of forgotten spaces into new public parks and civic commons. As more and more people live in dense urban areas around the world, the demand for new public spaces has grown dramatically. The Berlin Tempelhof airport, built in 1927 and one of Europe's most iconic pre-World War II airports, was a central hub for the Nazi war effort and later served as the staging area of the Berlin Airlift in 1948. After its closure to air travel in 2008, and following vociferous opposition to private development, local officials agreed in 2014 to allow the massive site to be used as Berlin's largest park, becoming a larger public venue than New York's Central Park. Indoor terminals and airport hangars were rendered usable, and the former runways are today freely accessible and highly popular for biking, sports, and public events. The decision to retain the disused infrastructure and simply reclaim the land for public use represents an emerging trend, which is explored further in a variety of examples in the final two chapters of this book. There is perhaps no greater testimony to the emotional value of abandoned architecture than this growing impulse to reclassify an abandoned site as a place that is valuable to the public, and usable as a communal gathering site.

War elicits enormous bloodshed and suffering, but it can also lead to the creation of memorable architecture. Certainly, military structures that make sense in wartime do so far less after the fighting stops. It is perhaps the strangeness of some of these structures that animates the imagination, and triggers an instinct to preserve them. Colossal bunkers were built by the Nazis in three strategic metropolitan areas across Germany and Austria, designed to shoot eight thousand rounds of anti-aircraft fire per minute from every direction while also serving as fully stocked shelters for civilians, complete with electricity, ventilated air, and potable water. While similar structures were repurposed across Europe after the war, flak towers in Vienna were left unused, leaving behind seemingly indestructible monuments.The British had built an eerie series of structures known as the Maunsell Sea Forts in the Thames Estuary to protect London during World War II. This cluster of seven fortified buildings rose from the sea on stilts; they were connected by an intricate network of catwalks, and were left abandoned after the war. While some of the sea forts were destroyed or have been repurposed, several remain today, standing like sentinels up to their "knees" in water. Multiple proposals and ideas have surfaced over the years for the creative reuse of these fascinating, often spooky structures. Here, it is not truly the beauty of the buildings that attract but rather their alienating effect. No longer useful from a military perspective, they retain their power and magic by inspiring a reimagination, and serving as haunting reminders of less peaceful times.

Yet buildings need not be militaristic to be terrifying. Sometimes, newly abandoned buildings can hide in plain sight, right in the center of our cities, inspiring wonder and awe. In the North Korean capital of Pyongyang, planners began a colossal tower in 1986 comprising three triangles, stretching 130 feet (40 meters) tall and containing roughly sixty-seven football-fields-worth of interior space—and

then abandoned it. This ill-fated Ryugyong Hotel, designed to compete with a South Korean skyscraper built in Singapore, faced construction and funding issues, which led to it remaining entirely empty despite its imposing impact on the city's skyline. In Caracas, Venezuela, a forty-five-story building was designed as a bank, but construction was halted due to financing issues in 1994. The abandoned structure, which housed roughly 2,500 squatters between 2007 and 2014, became known as the Torre de David, the world's tallest vertical slum—complete with its own electrical grid for indigent residents.

Abandoned entertainment venues offer an interesting narrative on changing cultural interests. In the southeastern U.S. state of Florida, the 6,500-seat Miami Marine Stadium was built in 1963, becoming the world's first venue for watching motorboat racing, along with concerts framed by a view of the downtown Miami skyline. In the wake of the devastating Hurricane Andrew in 1992, the coastal stadium was deemed unsafe and left abandoned, becoming a popular destination for graffiti artists. After being listed by the National Trust for Historic Preservation as one of the United States' eleven Most Endangered Historic Places in 2009, a group called Friends of Miami Marine Stadium led efforts to preserve and reclaim the building, leading to official city support for their effort in 2017. More transient examples of abandoned event venues are former Olympic Villages— designed for one period of intense activity, without a clear plan for sustained use. While abandoned Olympic venues pepper the globe, the 2004 Olympic Village in Athens, Greece, offers a recent example of what remains after athletes and spectators go home: rust, weeds, and graffiti. Perhaps it is precisely because Olympic Villages are built hastily, with such a focus on welcoming global visitors instead of considering local community interests, that many of these new structures fail to generate the emotional pull of venues that were traditionally popular among locals. Abandoned Olympic structures cry out to the visitor, serving as reminders of those moments, all too brief, when the world comes together to celebrate extraordinary feats of human strength and skill.

Left in place, anachronistic yet strangely reassuring, forgotten structures haunt us while reminding us of a bygone era. These buildings and their attendant spaces are in an exciting but precarious position: they have inspired interest, and in some cases preliminary funding or planning permission, but their fates are altogether uncertain. They fascinate, inspire and attract visitors— whether these are paying tourists, trespassers with cans of spray paint, or the homeless seeking refuge. A forgotten structure forces us to confront not merely the loss of its intended original use but also the wide range of potential future uses. Some will visit these spaces and recommend a good cleaning or a redesign, or an attempt to restore them to their former glory. For others, the quiet desolation of a dilapidated, forgotten, empty space offers a brief respite from the overly developed, relentlessly consumerist, brutally efficient worlds that we inhabit. Sometimes it is beautiful to forget something, even if only for a little while.

Miami Marine Stadium
Miami, FL, USA
Hilario Candela
Completed 1963
Abandoned 1992

△ Along the Florida coastline,and with a dramatic view of the downtown Miami skyline, the 6,500-seat Miami Marine Stadium was built as the world's first venue for watching motorboat racing, as well as concerts.

▽ ▷ After the devastating effects of Hurricane Andrew in 1992, the coastal stadium was deemed unsafe and abandoned. The Friends of Miami Marine Stadium group led efforts to preserve and reclaim it, leading to official city support for the effort in 2017.

Power Plant IM
Charleroi, Belgium
State Architect
Completed 1921
Abandoned 2007

△ Built as a cooling tower for a Belgian coal burning plant, the Monceau cooling tower featured a soaring cylindrical shape and geometric patterns, serving as the main source of energy for the surrounding area.

∇ Closed after reports of unacceptable carbon dioxide emissions, the tower remains a popular destination for explorers of abandoned spaces, despite demolition of the adjacent power plant.

**Buzludzha Monument
Kazanlak, Bulgaria
Georgi Stoilov
Completed 1974
Abandoned 1989**

△ In the Balkan mountains of central Bulgaria, on the site of a meeting of socialist philosophers in 1891, this monument was built to celebrate socialist communism. The spaceship-sized concrete saucer held large statues and murals of Lenin and Marx, with a vast tower next to the saucer, adorned with a massive Soviet star.

▽ Abandoned after the fall of the Soviet Union, the site has been largely left to the elements and to vandalism, remaining a fascinating, ghost-like point of interest for communist-inspired architecture lovers and ruin explorers.

Olympic Stadium
Athens, Greece
Santiago Calatrava
Completed 2004
Abandoned 2004

Δ Having hosted the first international modern Olympics Games in the year 1896, the city spent nearly 8.8 billion Euros (US$10.2 billion) for its second turn as host in 2004, engaging architect Santiago Calatrava to design a stunning new stadium with a retractable glass roof.

∇ As is the case with other former Olympic sites, many of the 2004 venues fell into years of disuse, disrepair, or neglect after the Games, prompting local criticism. The cost of the 2004 Olympic Games for the government of Greece has been cited as a factor contributing to the Greek public debt crisis since 2009.

Ryugyong Hotel
Pyongyang, North Korea
Baikdoosan Architects
Completed 1992
Abandoned 1992

△ To compete with a South Korean-built skyscraper in Singapore, North Korean officials built a colossal hotel tower comprising three glass wings, stretching 1,080 feet (330 meters) tall and containing roughly sixty-seven football fields of interior space. It was then abandoned, unfinished, several years later.

▽ Construction halted on the Ryugyong Hotel in 1992 due to funding issues and several unsuccessful attempts at completion. The project remains entirely empty, despite its imposing impact on the city's skyline, earning it the title of "tallest unoccupied building in the world."

PECO Delaware Station
Philadelphia, PA, USA
Windrim and Eglin
Completed 1916
Abandoned 1924

△ With Beaux-Arts facades and Romanesque details, the five-acre (two-hectare) coal-fired power plant facing the Delaware River heralded a high point for the manufacturing industry in Philadelphia, with a grand turbine hall, large boilers, and electrical rooms.

▽ Abandoned in 1924, the station has been used as a film set for a variety of movies, and was added to the National and Philadelphia Registers for Historic Places. Private owners have expressed interest in its possible transformation into an event venue.

Michigan Central Station
Detroit, MI, USA
Reed and Stern
Completed 1914
Abandoned 1988

△ The eighteen-story Beaux-Arts terminal was designed by Reed and Stern, in association with Warren and Wetmore. A symbol of the economic dominance of Detroit during the first decades of the automobile age, it served as a key train hub for seven decades but was decommissioned in 1988 due to declining use.

▽ Despite broad preservation efforts, the structure remained under threat of demolition for decades. In an interesting twist, the Ford Motor Company has announced plans to redevelop the stunning ruin, in partnership with local government—part of broader local economic development.

Glenwood Power Plant
Yonkers, NY, USA
Reed and Stern
Completed 1907
Abandoned 1968

△ To provide electrical energy for the New York Central Railroad, the Romanesque-Revival style power plant was built seven miles north of New York, along the Hudson River. It featured massive smokestacks and a grand turbine hall spanning 17,000 square feet (1,580 square meters) and standing 110 feet (34 meters) high.

▽ ▷ In 1963 as its turbines became outdated, the power station was decommissioned and shortly after was entirely abandoned. By the 2000s, the dilapidated site earned a reputation for violence, graffiti, and gang activity. Developer Lela Goren purchased the plant in 2012, with plans to create a cultural and shopping destination.

Tempelhof Airport
Berlin, Germany
Ernst Sagebiel
Completed 1923
Abandoned 2008

△ Before World War II, Tempelhof was one of Europe's busiest airports. It became a central hub for the Nazi war effort, and later served as the staging area of the 1948 Berlin Airlift. The site includes one of the world's largest terminal buildings, elaborate subterranean tunnels, and a giant canopy roof.

▽ After closure to air travel in 2008, and following vociferous opposition to private development, in 2014 the massive site began to be transformed into Berlin's largest park, Tempelhofer Feld. Indoor terminals and airport hangars were rendered usable, and the former runways are now freely accessible for public use.

Summer Olympic Village
Wustermark, Germany
State Architect
Completed 1936
Abandoned 1992

△ Built two years before the Nazi party came to power, the Olympic village construction was overseen by Reich Chancellor Adolf Hitler and included an elaborate complex to house four thousand international athletes, alongside training facilities, event venues, and a swimming pool.

▽ The village was used as a hospital for German soldiers during World War II, before being repurposed as a military barracks for Soviet soldiers until the early 1990s. The site has been abandoned and generally derelict since then, although there have been various ideas to repurpose it.

Gunkanjima Island
Japan
Mitsubishi Corporation
Completed 1890
Abandoned 1974

△ On an island off the coast of Japan near Nagasaki, the Mitsubishi Corporation operated a prolific coal-mining facility, which grew to support meteoric Japanese industrial growth. Dense housing complexes, surrounded by a protective sea wall, accommodated many thousands of Korean slave laborers until the end of World War II.

∇ Abandoned abruptly in the mid-seventies, the "ghost town" of concrete buildings earned the nickname "Battleship Island" due its resemblance to an armored warship. It was entirely untouched for decades, but opened to tourists in 2009, and added to the UNESCO World Heritage List in 2015.

InTempo Building
Benidorm, Spain
Pérez-Guerras Arquitectos
Completed 2014
Abandoned 2014

△ An unusually shaped forty-seven-story edifice with an M-shaped arch, the InTempo building was designed as the tallest residential structure in Spain. It features two towers 61 feet (19 meters) apart, linked from the thirty-eighth floor by a funnel-shaped connector.

▽ The building remained unoccupied despite its completion since 2014, due to construction and debt related issues. It has become a high profile symbol of the challenges associated with banking and development industries in Spain.

**Presidio Modelo
Nueva Gerona, Cuba
State Architect
Completed 1928
Abandoned 1966**

∆ Built by order of President Gerardo Machado as a "model prison" for political dissidents, these five panopticon structures were oriented around an obscured watchtower at the center, blackened out to create a sense of omnipresent, omnidirectional surveillance.

∇ The buildings were closed as a prison in the mid-sixties, following a period of overcrowding and riots. The site is now open to visitors as a museum and monument, attracting attention both for its most well known inmate, Fidel Castro, and the unusual panopticon design of the structure.

Olympic Park
Sarajevo, Bosnia
Boreisa Bouchard
Completed 1984
Abandoned 1992

△ When the Winter Olympics were held in Sarajevo in the region of Bosnia-Herzegovina, then Yugoslavia, a stunning series of venues for the games was erected, including vertiginous ski jumps, three-kilometer bobsled runs, and shiny medal podiums. It was the first communist country to host the winter games.

▽ Abandoned after the Olympics, the site witnessed widespread ethnic violence during the Bosnian War from 1992 until 1996, leaving it in a devastated condition. Alongside moss, graffiti, weeds, bullet holes, shelling remains, and remnant land mines, portions of the bobsled and luge tracks have been partially renovated.

**Flak Tower
Vienna, Austria
State Architect
Completed 1943
Abandoned 1946**

△ Among the Nazi defences built during World War II in key cities of Berlin, Hamburg, and Vienna, flak towers could shoot eight thousand rounds of anti-aircraft fire per minute from every direction, reaching distances of eight miles (fourteen kilometers), while also serving as bunkers.

▽ Abandoned after the war, demolition of the towers was deemed impossible both due to the hulking mass of the structures and the proximity to nearby residents, prompting a variety of repurposing ideas.

**Torre de David
Caracas, Venezuela
Enrique Gómez
Incomplete
Abandoned 1994**

△ This forty-five-story building was designed as a bank, and despite its near completion, construction was halted due to financing issues in the mid-nineties. Sliding into decline, the site would gradually come to be occupied by roughly 2,500 squatters, known as the Torre de David.

▽ In an attempt to eradicate what became the world's tallest vertical slum, local government officials relocated the abandoned tower's squatting residents in 2014. Despite multiple attempts to redevelop the property, it remained unused, incomplete, and in disrepair as of 2018.

Maunsell Sea Forts
Thames Estuary, England
Guy Maunsell
Completed 1942
Abandoned 1946

△ The British built an eerie series of structures known as the Maunsell Sea Forts in the Thames Estuary to protect London during World War II. These three clusters of seven fortified buildings rose from the sea on stilts and were connected by an intricate network of catwalks, but were abandoned after the war.

∇ ▷ While one of the sea forts was destroyed, others have been temporarily repurposed, and two sea forts remain today, standing like sentinels up to their knees in water. There have been multiple proposals for the creative reuse of these fascinating structures; so far they remain in a rusty, dreamlike derelict state.

Restaurante Panorâmico
Lisbon, Portugal
Chaves da Costa
Completed 1968
Abandoned 2001

△ Sitting 820 feet (250 meters) above Lisbon, in the vast Monsanto Forest Park, this circular restaurant was built to offer panoramic views of the city below, encased by large omnidirectional glass windows set in faceted concrete panels.

▽ Abandoned just after the millennium, its winding staircases emphasize the ruin's aura of romance and grandeur. It has become such a favorite spot for urban adventurers and tourists that in 2017 the city funded a rehabilitation that allows guests to visit safely.

Council of Ministries
Sukhumi, Georgia
State Architect
Completed 1960s
Abandoned 1993

△ An example of Brutalist architecture, this grand government building became a symbol of the significance of Sukhumi in the Soviet era. The region's warm climate and its beaches along the Black Sea served as an elite summer getaway.

▽ In the wake of the fall of the Soviet Union, the building was badly damaged. It was entirely abandoned after heavy fighting in the disputed Abkhazia region during the 1992–93 armed conflict and remains uninhabited.

Lost

Reimagined

Trilateral Wadden Sea World
Heritage Partnership Center
Wilhelmshaven, Germany
Dorte Mandrup Arkitekter

St Peter's
Cardross, Scotland
Avanti Architects, ERZ
Landscape Architects,
McGinlay Bell Architects

River LA
Los Angeles, CA, USA
Frank Gehry, and teams

Lowline
New York, NY, USA
Raad Studio

Villa Zarri Experiential
Beer Garden
Castel Maggiore, Italy
DANA

QueensWay
New York, NY, USA
WXY and DLANDstudio

Atlanta BeltLine
Atlanta, GA, USA
Ryan Gravel, Perkins + Will

11th Street Bridge Park
Washington, D.C., USA
OMA and OLIN

Chongqing Museum and
Creative Industry Park
Chongqing, China
Avanti Architects

Forgotten

Encountering an abandoned space and imagining a new future for it is perhaps a natural impulse for creative thinkers and design enthusiasts. It may be the form that attracts and inspires reimagining: *What could we do with an Egyptian-style pyramid, built in the 1980s in an Eastern European capital?* It may be the haunting original function that most instantly appeals: *How can we repurpose the only bunker in a seaside city to survive World War II?* In other cases, it is the intended future purpose of a dilapidated structure that serves as the inspiration—turning something ugly or useless into something inspiring and valuable, or a new civic idea or concept that solves a contemporary urban problem.

Often, this can be the end of the story: the viewer encounters a site that resonates in some way, and imagines a new use for it; if truly inspired, the idea may be explored but then dismissed as too difficult or distracting. But sometimes, an individual, an organization, or a government entity turns an inspired transformation idea into a viable proposal. This step is not easily taken. It requires considerable curiosity and focus, and a profound understanding of the original structure, its history, and current contextual constraints. It requires comprehensive insight into any local, political perspectives on the structure, and on the intended purpose of the reimagined space. It necessitates building a community of supporters, slowly growing a circle of key stakeholders who firmly believe that the project should move ahead.

It also requires cash. In order to turn any of these ideas into actions, someone needs to underwrite the initial ideation process—or be willing to volunteer the time and energy needed to help formulate a clear idea. In order to be taken seriously by potential funders, this initial articulation of the vision requires some kind of official study or feasibility report related to the proposed transformation, leading to a sophisticated technical proposal and a carefully calculated capital-budget estimate. Early on, it can also be helpful to render compelling images to help various stakeholders understand and personally connect with the idea in a visual way.

This is a delicate moment in any transformation process. Whoever pays for the development of an idea often has a passionate and vested interest in its coming to fruition in the way it was initially envisioned. In order to move ahead, it must push aside or argue against other potential uses of the abandoned space. A key question here is how and to what extent local community residents, who arguably will be most impacted by a design intervention, are included in the ideation and design process. Often, it is easier for designers to assume that communities will merely thank them for the beautiful new structures in their backyards, without regard to the potentially negative or unintended consequences of newly redesigned sites. It is perhaps an arrogant proposition to assert one clear vision to transform an abandoned space when there are several other, very different, potential uses for it. Land use is always political. The challenge is to use this arrogant creativity to highlight an idea, build consensus for a

permutation of that idea, incorporate real feedback into it, and then refine it in a way that allows the broader community to truly feel and be involved. Not all projects get this right.

In this survey of abandoned projects with viable redesign proposals, an emerging trend is the reimagination of disused transportation infrastructure in major metropolitan areas. In what has been termed "the High Line effect," abandoned railroad lines, highways, bridges, and even waterways have been reimagined worldwide as new public spaces, citing as inspiration the highly successful High Line park in New York. Many of these projects share a common vision of becoming vibrant, welcoming, green spaces, and are propelled via nonprofit advocacy organizations that marshal private and public support; build platforms for grassroots community input; and lead programming, maintenance, and operations alongside city entities. In each case, these efforts push forward new ways of looking at what constitutes valuable real estate, and focus on reclaiming these spaces for public rather than commercial use. While the initial structures may never have been designed for, or even considered anything other than technically useful for, transportation purposes, these newly reclaimed spaces become bright, new marvels of architectural and landscape design.

The beautiful decay of many of these locations certainly inspires their "unofficial" reuse as spray-painting meccas; urban-explorer adventure zones; communal space; temporary shelter; or less savory, even criminal activities. Then there are often multiple "official" proposals for the sites—ranging from demolition to new creative or commercial functions, to reusing the site for precisely what it was used for in an earlier era. But if it were possible to wind back the clock and return the site to its former use, the space would likely not have been abandoned in the first place. The priorities of neighborhoods and cities never remain constant. Nostalgia may inspire their preservation, but the human need for something new is what often inspires the reimagination of abandoned sites.

Numerous potential pitfalls face any proposed redesign project—from expensive construction delays to the shifting winds of local politics, to an inability to raise timely capital funding. Projects with clear and committed public or private ownership and comprehensive funding at the outset generally have the greatest likelihood of becoming built, on time and at the most efficient cost. Even when the stars seem to align—funding is in place, public support is unwavering, an inspiring design is ready for construction—it is always possible that any of these fascinating concepts may, for one reason or another, not come to fruition.

Years from now, some of these projects will have opened to the public to great fanfare, and others may be relegated to bittersweet, unrequited architectural fantasies. But here we imagine what is possible, what has been both dreamed and designed, and what is on the table for serious consideration by funders; developers; and, perhaps most importantly, adjacent communities.

Prussian Navy Bunker
Wilhelmshaven, Germany
Completed 1853
Abandoned 1945

Trilateral Wadden Sea
World Heritage
Partnership Center
Dorte Mandrup Arkitekter
Reimagined 2018

△ Disused navy yards on the German coast
of the Wadden Sea, an area later recognized
as a globally significant coastal wetlands.

In 1853, the Prussian Navy built a bunker on the Wadden Sea on the northwest German coast, in an area that would become known as Wilhelmshaven. It was used in World War II to provide protection from attacks. Amid heavy bombing during the conflict, the bunker was among the few remaining buildings in the city by the war's end, and the building was decommissioned but used informally by the German Navy. By the twentieth century, the Wadden Sea area became increasingly recognized for its significance as one of the most important intertidal ecosystems in the world, although the site of the former bunker had been identified as having been contaminated during World War II. The Wadden Sea coastline, stretching from Denmark to Germany to the Netherlands, is an important site for migratory birds, home to endemic gray seals, and one of the world's largest contiguous coastal wetlands, with mudflats popular for hiking. In 2009, the region was placed on the UNESCO World Heritage List.

In 2017, the City of Wilhelmshaven launched a design competition to transform the abandoned bunker into a new office building for a joint Danish, German, and Dutch company focused on protecting and preserving the Wadden Sea area. Funded by the German Government, the competition received fourteen proposals, leading to the selection of Dorte Mandrup Arkitekter. The Danish architect's proposal directly integrates the bunker into the design of the new office building, with minimal intervention. This approach means that the new building requires as little land as possible, allowing the surrounding area to be untouched or used for other purposes.

In the new design, four stories of spaces for offices, conference areas, and technical research will be added above the former building, and then entirely wrapped by a double-glazed glass facade. The top floors will include terraces overlooking the coastline of the Wadden Sea, with a staircase connecting to the side entrance of the bunker. By day, the glass facade will mirror the reflective surface of the Wadden Sea, while at night the glass "box" will act as a glowing lighthouse. The old bunker remains visible on the ground level, and will be transformed into a space for exhibitions, events, and archives. Rainwater will be captured in an organically shaped surface surrounding the structure, which will also act as simple spaces in which to gather on sunny days.

Reflecting trilateral cooperation between the three countries sharing a coastline along the Wadden Sea, the new building in Wilhelmshaven will form one third of the Trilateral Wadden Sea World Heritage Partnership Center. Two additional wings of the centre will be based in Germany's two partner countries: in Ribe, on Denmark's west coast, which opened in 2017; and in Lauwersoog, in the Netherlands. All three buildings have been designed by Dorte Mandrup, unifying the overall project as a design "trilogy."

The new building in Wilhelmshaven, slated to open by 2020, offers a fresh chapter in the preservation of the natural beauty and ecological significance of the Wadden Sea while also preserving an important symbol of the region's maritime and naval history.

△ One of the only remaining buildings to survive World War II, the concrete bunker was left to decay for decades.

▽ The new design for the World Heritage Center preserves the bunker at its core, wrapped by a glass facade.

◁ A double-glazed skin will reflect the Wadden Sea surface by day.

▷ ▽ Exploded axonometric and section illustrating the four new levels of office, conference and research facilities. The bunker will house exhibitions, events, and an archive.

▽ Site plan showing the complex, adjacent to the Wadden Sea.

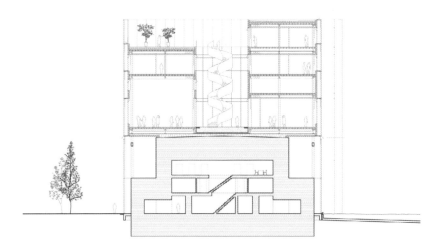

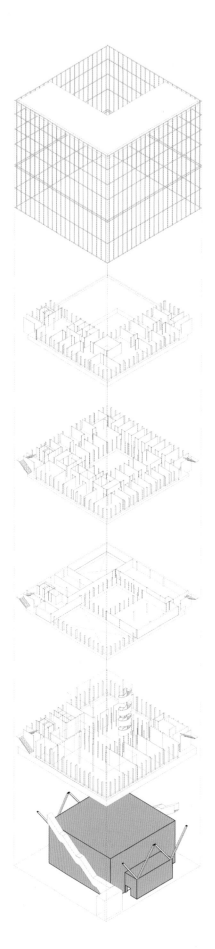

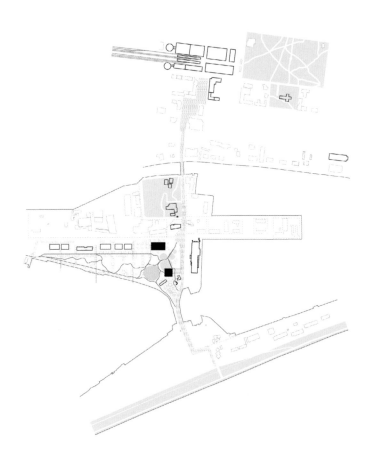

St. Peter's Seminary
Gillespie, Kidd & Coia
Cardross, Scotland
Completed 1966
Abandoned 1987

St Peter's
Avanti Architects, ERZ
Landscape Architects,
McGinlay Bell
Reimagined 2006–

△ Historic view of St Peter's Seminary showing the primary accommodation quarters, and entry, left, and the cantilevered teaching block, right.

Situated 20 miles (32 kilometers) outside Glasgow in the forests of Cardross, Argyll and Bute, St. Peter's Seminary was built in the 1960s, immediately earning its spot among Scotland's most admired and celebrated modern buildings. Inspired by the raw beauty of Scotland's landscape and the modern Brutalism of Le Corbusier, the design firm of Gillespie, Kidd & Coia built a quadrangle of concrete blocks around a nineteenth-century mansion, Kilmahew House, to provide temporary housing for priests entering the Catholic Church. Completed in 1966 the 140 acre (57 hectare) seminary compound merged the seclusion and grandeur of the Catholic Church with a Modernist optimism expressed in mid-century architecture. The new building had the capacity to provide housing for a hundred students, along with reserved areas for professors, classrooms, and a convent.

Yet as the Catholic Church's approach edged further away from social isolation and closer to immersion with communities, the need for the complex declined. Its housing quarters were never entirely filled, and the cool buildings suffered insulation and maintenance issues. The

Archdiocese of Glasgow had closed the seminary by 1980. It served briefly as a drug rehabilitation center in the 1980s but soon shut all operations, becoming completely derelict by the 1990s despite its widespread acknowledgment as a gem of Modernist architecture. Graffiti artists took over the gray blocks, leaving colorful marks where glass and plaster had once stood. In 1992, the conservation body Historic Scotland listed the former seminary building as a "Category A" historical site, but that did not prevent a 1995 fire from burning down the historic Kilmahew House.

In 2007 the site was added to the World Monuments Fund's list of most endangered sites. That same year, NVA, a Glasgow-based public arts organization, began exploring a potential reuse for the site, alongside local community organizations. Hoping to transform the former seminary building into a vibrant public space for the creative arts, NVA worked with Avanti and ERZ Landscape Architects to reveal the bones of the building, removing the effects of years of neglect to make way for performance and event spaces, and has secured £7 million ($9.3 million) in funding for redesign, weatherproofing,

and preliminary construction, with help from the Heritage Lottery Fund, Creative Scotland, artists, and the community. In March 2016, with the support of NVA, the former seminary hosted the launch of Scotland's year-long Festival of Architecture, in a sold-out, immersive light-and-sound installation entitled *Hinterland*. Architectural plans would transform the three-story chapel into a large event venue, with other spaces used for exhibitions, and a landscape design bringing the entire estate together through newly installed pathways, bridges, and gardens.

While funding challenges have led to an unclear fate for the redesign effort, the Archdiocese of Glasgow, which still retains ownership of the site, has remained committed to the idea of a noncommercial future for the space. If the NVA plan is ultimately realized, the revamped site would serve as a very different kind of refuge, transforming from an isolated seminary into a cultural hub and "magnet," inviting people from around the world to celebrate creativity in a unique public setting.

△ The abandoned main block before renovation in 2016, complete with graffiti and decay.

▽ Model of proposed new restoration with ziggurat-like frame by McGinlay Bell.

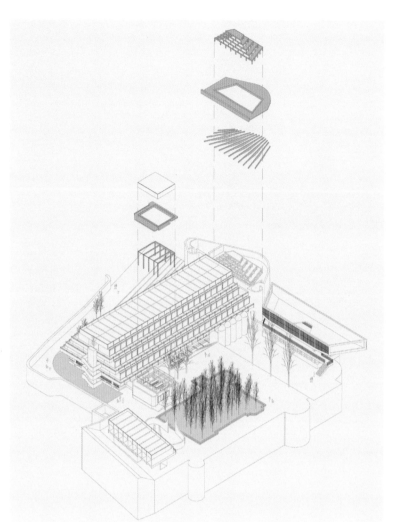

◁ McGinlay Bell's proposed axonometric showing new designed interventions alongside partial restorations.

▷ Proposed views of the exterior of St Peter's by McGinlay Bell, and interior of the restored chapel by Avanti Architects.

▽ View of the proposed masterplan to regenerate the landscape of the seminary and larger Kilmahew estate by ERZ.

Los Angeles River
Los Angeles, CA, USA
U.S. Army Corps
Completed 1913
Abandoned 1938

River LA
Frank Gehry and teams
Reimagined 2016

△ Today the Los Angeles River is broadly inaccessible to local residents.

▷ A view of the disused Los Angeles River snaking through the city, paved in concrete.

While visitors to Los Angeles may never notice it, a long river runs through the sprawling city—and, indeed, led to its development. The Los Angeles River covers nearly 51 miles (82 kilometers), stretching southeast from the San Fernando Valley to Long Beach. Despite running dry for large parts of the year, and periodically flooding during intense rain, the river was used for centuries as a source of water and food, and served as the primary water source for the Los Angeles Basin until 1913. After suffering a disastrous flood, killing over a hundred people in 1938, the City of Los Angeles enlisted the U.S. Army Corps of Engineers to pave the river entirely with concrete, leaving behind a barren, bleak storm drain. For decades, the only liquid trickling through this channel was polluted run-off from local factories.

Toward the end of the twentieth century, various groups focused on ways of reclaiming the waterway for public use—including Friends of the Los Angeles River (FOLAR), founded in 1986. In 2007, the engineering firm Tetra Tech completed a revitalization master plan, which was approved by the LA City Council after over two hundred stakeholder meetings. In 2009,

the city established the LA River Revitalization Corporation, which grew into a new organization, River LA. In 2014, the River LA team approached architect Frank Gehry to further develop the master plan. Although not a landscape designer, Gehry was an LA resident interested in the long term viability of the city; he agreed to collaborate in order to reconsider water issues, sustainability, and local resilience. Bringing in landscape practice OLIN and engineering firm Geosyntec, the group developed preliminary plans and 3-D models to reopen the riverbanks to public use, while reimagining and reusing the existing concrete infrastructure.

In 2016, LA City Council approved "Alternative 20," a plan to transform 11 miles (17.7 kilometers) of the river near the city's downtown by removing concrete from its bed, at an estimated cost of over $1 billion. The plan would connect downtown Los Angeles with Griffith Park to the north and introduce new wetlands to manage stormwater runoff and improve the river's ecological well-being, allowing for the recycling of gallons of otherwise wasted water. In 2017, the State of California pledged $100 million and the City

of Los Angeles devoted $365 million for construction of bike paths. Notably, fees from local real estate developers along the redevelopment route would help to provide additional funding over time.

River LA is now focused on creating Greenway 2020, a vision for a continuous "greenway" and bike paths for the entire length of the river, stitching various neighborhoods to downtown and to each other. As the Gehry-led design team prepare to unveil new visions for the river in 2018, it is clear that the ambitious project faces significant challenges: building consensus among dozens of different neighborhoods, securing additional funding, and restoring natural ecosystems after years of neglect. Yet if successful, it may be one of the most ecologically impactful modern examples of transforming infrastructure—an opportunity to invite nature, and public use, back to the Los Angeles River.

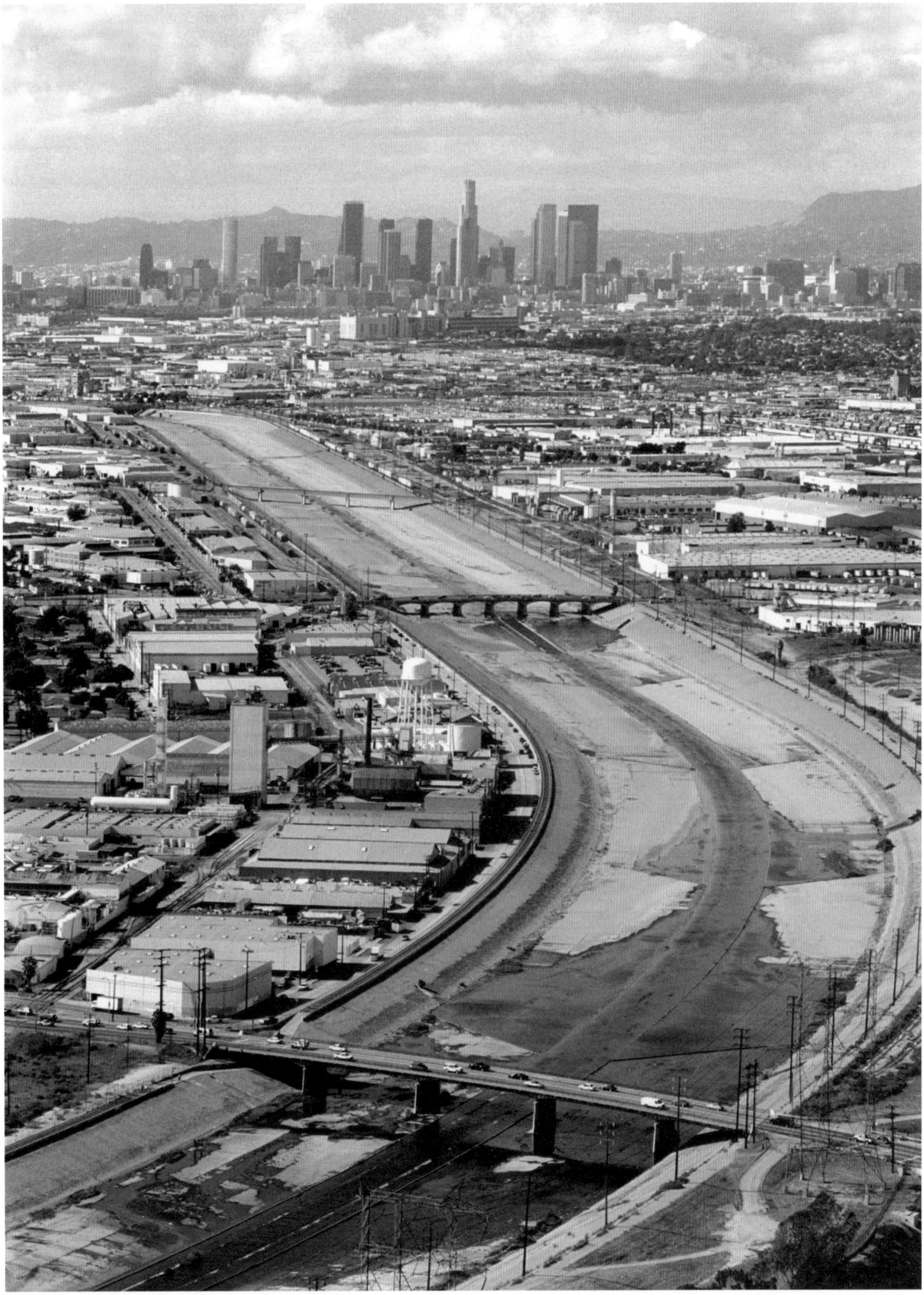

7

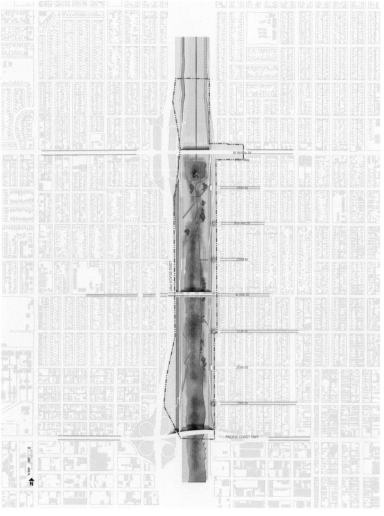

◁ Drawings envision weaving the river back into the local community, providing multiple access points and rebuilding the local ecosystem.

▽ Green, planted ribbons interspersed along the riverfront, allow visitors to interact with the waterway anew.

▷ Initial views of the revised scheme juxtapose natural elements alongside concrete, giving new social uses for local residents.

Williamsburg Bridge Trolley Terminal
New York, NY, USA
Completed 1908
Abandoned 1948

Lowline
Raad Studio
Reimagined 2011

△ The former trolley terminal in the 1930s, where passengers embarked for travel over the newly built Williamsburg Bridge.

8

In the early twentieth century New York's Lower East Side was among the most densely populated neighborhoods on the planet, with huge influxes of immigrants from Eastern Europe packed into tight tenements. When the new Williamsburg Bridge was constructed to connect the area to Brooklyn, planners built subterranean trolley-car terminals at either side of the bridge to facilitate public transit. On the Manhattan side a 60,000 square foot (5,600 square meter) underground terminal was opened in 1908, spanning three city blocks below busy Delancey Street. Passengers embarked and disembarked in this underground station for four decades, until the trolley system was decommissioned in 1948. The underground site was left entirely abandoned, adjacent to and across from subway tracks that would become the new J/M/Z subway line. Through the neighborhood's mid- and late-century decline, the space remained vacant for decades, used mainly by graffiti artists and urban nomads.

In 2009 a local architectural designer, James Ramsey, learned of the abandoned space from a former transit official and became inspired by its potential. The football-field-sized area retained its original Belgian block details, trolley-car tracks, overhead catenary tracks, and vaulted ceilings—and lay just below the sidewalks of the still-crowded Lower East Side. His design firm, Raad Studio, was separately exploring lighting solutions that could deliver natural sunlight below ground using advanced optical technology, allowing plants and greenery to grow underground or in locations lacking solar access. He and partner Dan Barasch collaborated to set up a not-for-profit organization, the Underground Development Foundation, exploring the idea of building an underground "park" in the former trolley terminal using this new technology. Initial backers nicknamed the project the "Lowline," since its transformative reuse narrative was reminiscent of the High Line project, which in 2009 had opened its first segment to much fanfare.

Launching the Lowline concept to the public in 2011 with preliminary renderings, the duo raised an initial $155,000 for research on crowdfunding platform Kickstarter—an unprecedented amount for public design. In 2012, the team opened a preliminary exhibition in a nearby abandoned warehouse, *Imagining the Lowline*, to showcase an initial version of the technology and the design sensibility. Following a second Kickstarter campaign in 2015, which again broke records, the Lowline Lab was opened to the public, attracting over 110,000 people to a working prototype of the design. Complete with three heliostatic collection and distribution systems, and over three thousand plants, it remained open until early 2017. Receiving public support from elected officials and local community groups, the Lowline received a conditional site designation from Mayor Bill de Blasio's administration in 2016.

Significant challenges face the project and its ability to bring the site to life, including the size and breakdown of its capital-funding model, the mechanics of delivering sunlight underground, and mitigating impacts on the adjacent subway. Yet the Lowline offers a new paradigm for both the concept of an urban park and the interplay of the city and nature itself. Its emergence has raised exciting prospects for underground development initiatives all over the world, reclaiming subterranean infrastructure as both worthy of preservation and ripe for creative reinvention for public use.

△ The abandoned site has become a favorite
haunt for local graffiti artists as well as subterranean adventurers.

▽ Initial plans by Raad imagine partitioning
the site into an open plaza, a verdant ramble,
and flexible spaces for meetings and gatherings.

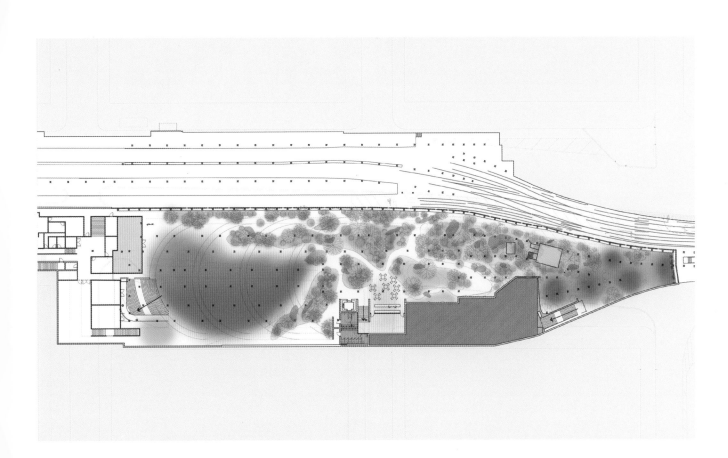

◁ The design includes a juxtaposition of existing rail lines and Belgian blocks with new greenery and pathways for exploration.

▽ The green space would be facilitated by optical technology, introducing reflected daylight, that allows for full-spectrum wavelengths of light- and therefore photosynthesis, underground.

▷ In an abandoned market building just blocks away from the Lowline site, the Lowline Lab tested the solar technology and landscape design in all four seasons, demonstrating the technical viability of the concept.

Villa Zarri
Castel Maggiore, Italy
Completed 1578
Abandoned 1990s

Villa Zarri Experiential
Beer Garden
DANA
Reimagined 2016

△ The abandoned distillery building, featuring a centralized space with unique curved roofs.

In the midst of the ancient Emilian landscape, on the road from the city of Bologna to northern Italy, a grand, Neo-Classical villa was built in 1578 for a noble family, and underwent significant restoration in the eighteenth century by the Marquis Nerio Lorenzo Pietro Angelelli. Situated in the town of Castel Maggiore, the central villa is surrounded on both sides by corridors that were once greenhouses. The grounds also included a chapel and vast gardens. After World War II Leonida Zarri purchased the site and redeveloped it into a distillery complex. By the end of the twentieth century Villa Zarri had become known as a significant producer of Italian brandy, distilled with Trebbanio grapes from the hillsides of Tuscany and Emilia-Romagna. Yet a key distillery building on the grounds fell into disuse, remaining abandoned for several years.

In 2016 Villa Zarri, keen to fuse its cultural focus on local production with a desire to create a modern and global cultural destination, focused on transforming its abandoned distillery into a new microbrewery and beer garden. Partnering with the Italian Association of Industrials and the Young Architects Competition, it led a

competitive design process for the transformation of several buildings on the site, and selected Spanish firm DANA to develop an "experiential beer garden." Inspired in part by the late-twentieth-century German tradition of beer gardens, the designers sought to transform the open, structurally intact distillery buildings, which had been gutted and were awash with natural sunlight via skylights. The objective was to merge the elegant, refined—even rustic—liveliness of the Italian villa into new social hubs with a modern, more social, beer-drinking sensibility.

The new design focused on three interventions within the abandoned site. First, a new, bold exterior entrance composed of gold-plated, perforated, metal plates, inspired by the bubbly appearance of a glass of beer, would attract visitors and signal a modern effect. Second, the building's interior would be transformed by the replacement of a northern wall with a large glazed facade, allowing for direct views to the lush gardens inside the old cellar and fostering both the open feeling of a beer garden and an appreciation of the villa's natural surroundings. And third, a new, curvilinear, metal roof built over

the gardens in the shape of its pathways would allow for a heightened ability for visitors to relax and enjoy the gardens while drinking the beer crafted on-site.

Aiming to build a "sanctuary" devoted both to nature and to the appreciation of beer, the Villa Zarri Experiential Beer Garden adds a layer of social mission to its operations. Appreciated for centuries for its beauty; elegance; and, more recently, for its brandy, this redesign may turn Villa Zarri into a new, global destination for an ancient yet freshly modern human luxury: the consumption of beer, among friends—with the added pleasure of being surrounded by the beauty and history of the northern Italian countryside.

△ Within the vaulted roofs lit by clerestory
lighting, the vast spans that once housed brandy
invited transformation into a microbrewery.

▽ Reimagined as a "sanctuary" devoted to
celebrating beer, the proposal opens the site
to its natural environment.

▷   A perforated golden metal plate creates an iconic new entrance, and a shaded *porte-cochère* for the historic building.

▽   The scalloped gold facade borrows from the preexisting curved rooftops of the original distillery building.

◁   ▽   Beyond the new exterior, which is evocative of bubbles of beer, lies an inviting landscaped inner courtyard.

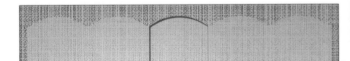

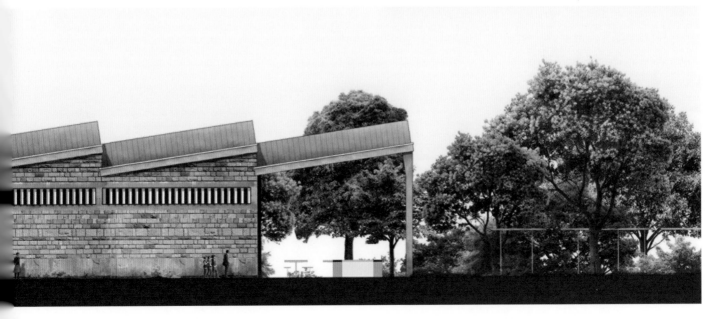

Rockaway Beach Branch
Long Island Rail Road
Queens, NY, USA
Completed 1880
Abandoned 1962

QueensWay
WXY and DLANDstudio
Reimagined 2013

△ A portion of the Long Island Rail Road in Queens, New York was abandoned in the early sixties when local transit planners removed investment in the site.

Built in 1880 as part of the Long Island Rail Road in the borough of Queens in New York, the Rockaway Beach Branch Line extended from the well-to-do suburb of Rego Park down into the Rockaway beachfront neighborhood. A fire on a train trestle in 1950 led to a series of track closures and a decline in maintenance for this portion of the rail line, which transit officials eventually abandoned by 1962. Over the next several decades the disused site became home to a great overgrowth of trees and plants alongside decaying trestles, discarded refuse, and rusty rail infrastructure. It also became known among locals as a derelict site and a magnet for crime. Multiple proposals surfaced for the potential transformation of the site, including several concepts related to the reuse of the elevated railway for new or reimagined public transit.

In 2005 local residents, inspired by the opening of the High Line in Manhattan, developed a proposal to transform their abandoned rail line into a community park and green space. Forming a nonprofit organization, Friends of the Queensway, the group partnered with the Trust for Public Land in 2011 to provide support and

advocacy for the idea. In 2013, the team hired architecture and planning firm WXY and landscape architecture firm DLANDstudio to conduct a study on the project's feasibility.

The overall goal of the project would be the creation of a 3.5 mile (5.6 kilometer) greenway spanning 47 acres (19 hectares), accessible to pedestrians and cyclists via walking trails and bike lanes. Planners envisioned multiple access points for the park at major intersections—effectively weaving six very different neighborhoods together and linking the borough to nearby green spaces, including Forest Park and Flushing Meadow Corona Park. In 2013 a New York State grant supported a series of community workshops and a schematic design from DLANDstudio. Released in May 2017 these initial designs for the first section of the proposed park included the development of new gardens, pedestrian and bicycle paths, and outdoor classrooms, to be used primarily by the over one hundred thousand local residents within a ten-minute walk of the QueensWay. The landscape design would retain much of the existing site conditions, including fifty-year-old trees and rusty rail tracks, offering a less

cultivated version of the High Line. The new park would also seek to restore healthy ecosystems, and to eliminate invasive plant species currently growing on the neglected site.

The QueensWay proposal, which aims to provide the borough of Queens with a green space that would not only serve local residents but perhaps also become a destination for nonresidents and an economic driver for the area, faces significant challenges. In a borough that lacks Manhattan's globally recognized cultural attractions, deep-pocketed real estate developers, or other influential stakeholders, the project has struggled to attract major public or private funding commitments. Some local residents are concerned about the potential displacement to be caused by a new destination park in their community, and transit advocates continue to support the former railway being repurposed for public-transportation projects.

△ Untouched for decades, the former rail lines snake their way through multiple neighborhoods.

▽ Greenery and trees have reclaimed much of the periphery alongside the tracks.

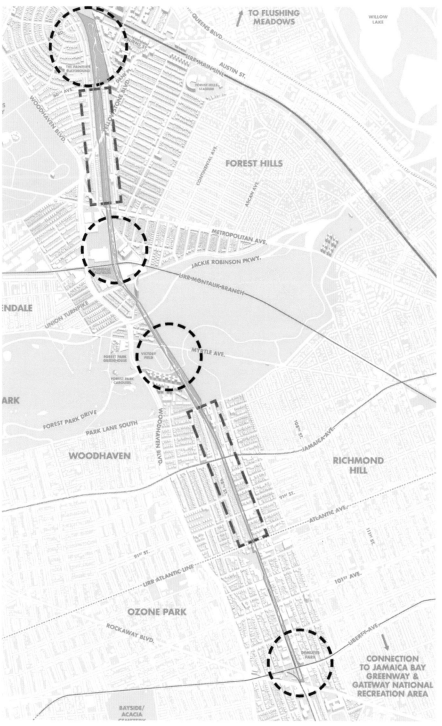

◁   Proposing to extend over a distance of 3.5 miles (5.6 kilometers), the Queensway would serve as a critical link to residential areas, city parks, and other community amenities.

▽   The abandoned rail lines include elevated portions, offering unique opportunities to interact with the streets and communities below.

▷   Proposals by WXY imagine a meandering reuse of the railways, incorporating both natural elements and linear passageways for pedestrians and cyclists.

Atlanta West Point Railroad
Atlanta, GA, USA
Completed 1870–1902
Abandoned 1980–2014

Atlanta BeltLine
Ryan Gravel, Perkins + Will
Reimagined 2005

△ The Atlanta railroad lines stretch an area encompassing twenty-two miles (thirty-five kilometers) throughout the metropolitan area.

From the 1870s to 1902 a series of railways was built in the city of Atlanta to support its role as a major rail hub of the southeastern United States. Rail lines connecting Atlanta with the cities of Richmond, Louisville, Nashville, and up and down the eastern seaboard were built in a ringlike fashion, circling the city. Different sections of this ring of railways were abandoned in the ensuing decades, leaving behind dozens of miles of disused pathways and thousands of acres of adjacent land.

In 1999, designer Ryan Gravel wrote his graduate shool thesis on the potential of transforming abandoned portions of the railway into an expansive public park, offering a highly urbanized Atlanta a vast new set of opportunities for communal meeting places. He distributed the thesis to several influential Atlantans; founded a nonprofit organization, Friends of the Belt Line; and, by 2004, had gained support from Atlanta's mayor, city council president, and local business leaders. In 2005 the Atlanta BeltLine Partnership was formed to lead the effort at the city level, with the full support of the Mayor's Office. City officials have included the BeltLine as a critical

component of Atlanta's long-term economic development strategy, with a vision of converting twenty-two miles (thirty-five kilometers) of former railway into multipurpose spaces—including footpaths, new light transit, and cycling routes—as part of its twenty-five-year Mobility 2030 strategy for the Atlanta metropolitan area. The plan will connect forty-five neighborhoods across Atlanta, opening communities up to each other in new ways, linked by a vibrant green space.

The first groundbreaking events for completed portions of the BeltLine were held in 2008, with additional segments opening to the public over the next decade. By 2017, over $450 million had been committed to the project from public and private sources, leading to over 9 miles (14.5 kilometers) of new trails and over 674 acres (273 hectares) of new and renewed green spaces or remediated brownfields. When complete, the $4.8 billion project will provide 2,000 new acres (809 hectares) of green space for Atlanta, in the form of an "emerald necklace" park system that encircles the city.

The BeltLine's impact on the city of Atlanta extends beyond the creation of public green

spaces. It has been an important center for the arts, hosting large scale art and performance installations and the annual BeltLine Lantern Parade since 2010. It has also been an important driver of affordable housing. After the Atlanta BeltLine pledged to build thousands of new units of affordable housing, Atlanta City Council approved legislation requiring new developers to build new affordable-housing units along its route. By directly addressing widespread concerns about the BeltLine's impact on raising real estate prices in adjacent neighborhoods, the project has developed real potential to help mitigate the displacement of vulnerable residents, and alleviate a critical low income-housing shortage. By simultaneously offering new green space, affordable housing opportunities, art and cultural events, and greener transportation alternatives, the BeltLine is transforming Atlanta from a city of disconnected suburban sprawl to a much more unified and livable place.

△ Largely abandoned, the lines weave through multiple neighborhoods and include a variety of infrastructural details.

▽ Portions of the former rail line have already been proposed or transformed into walkways.

◁ The project has the potential to weave together a substantial number of Atlanta neighborhoods via a contiguous green belt that would span the city.

◁ Aerial view of the Eastside Trail, the first finished section of the BeltLine, designed for cycle and pedestrian use.

▷ ▽ While portions of the BeltLine have been converted into walking trails, bike paths, and greenways, the effort to reclaim the entire structure is ongoing.

11th Street Bridge
Washington, D.C., USA
Completed 1965
Abandoned 2012

11th Street Bridge Park
OMA and OLIN
Reimagined 2016

Δ   The disused 11th Street Bridge spans the Anacostia River, connecting Washington D.C.'s Navy Yard with the Anacostia neighborhood.

The 11th Street Bridges—a series of three crossings built over the Anacostia River in Washington, D.C.—were completed in 1965, but by 2009 required significant structural updates, improvements and repairs in order to keep pace with anticipated traffic demands. In the midst of this rehabilitation of a critical infrastructure corridor, the District of Columbia Department of Transportation (DDOT) initially planned to demolish those parts of the bridge spans that were not slated for car traffic, transforming them instead into overlooks and fishing piers. However, by 2012, the D.C. Mayor's Office of Planning, inspired by the success of the High Line in New York, proposed retaining the disused structures and transforming them into an elevated park. The vision was centered on an opportunity to support the economy and improve residents' well-being on the Anacostia side of the bridge, home to Ward 8, one of the lowest-income neighborhoods in the city.

Partnering with Building Bridges Across the River at THEARC (Washington's Town Hall Education Arts Recreation Campus), a nonprofit organization serving the needs of the surrounding area, and 11th Street Bridge Park, a new organization focused specifically on the project, the city supported an ambitious community engagement process to ensure that the future park not only met the highest standards of design excellence but also improved nearby neighborhoods while protecting vulnerable populations. Hundreds of community meetings brought together a diversity of local residents and other stakeholders, culminating in an Equitable Development Plan that laid out specific objectives related to the workforce, small-business support, and affordable-housing preservation. The team raised over $1.5 million to pursue this work, and an additional $50 million in direct investment to local organizations focused on the implementation of the plan.

The team then held a seven-month design competition in order to develop proposals for the transformation of the old bridge into a new public space. OMA and OLIN were selected as the design firm in 2014, with a vision for Anacostia Crossing, a series of connecting pathways for a wide range of amenities, to be built on the pillars of the old road bridge. It would be financed and supported with both city funding and private support. Once complete, the 11th Street Bridge Park would cover a space roughly the size of three U.S. football fields, or three acres (1.2 hectares).

Preliminary construction on the park began in 2016 and it is estimated to open as early as 2019. Residents on either side of the Anacostia River will clearly benefit from this design intervention, with the creation of new outdoor attractions, recreational facilities, and community programs. 11th Street Bridge Park is among the first projects of its kind, however, in its consistent focus on physically and culturally weaving two communities together. It seeks to harness all of the power of a new public space, becoming both an inspiring reuse of abandoned infrastructure and a far-reaching, sustainable catalyst for equitable development within a vulnerable community.

△ OMA and OLIN's designs weave the bridge into the surrounding vicinity of the waterfront with an ambitious green design.

▽ The reimagined bridge structure takes full advantage of its access to the sky and includes stunning outdoor venues.

◁ A series of voids along the bridge creates spaces for play and river access. Both the performance space and café are partially cut into the bridge, creating recessed zones with river views.

▽ The Anacostia paths join to form a loop, linking the opposing banks in a single gesture: an iconic "X" that is an instantly recognizable form in the river.

◁ To encourage use of the bridge in all seasons, including winter, the proposal includes places that provide warmth, refreshment, and amenity along its entire length.

Chongqing Iron and Steelworks
Chongqing, China
Completed 1938
Abandoned 2006

Chongqing Museum and Creative Industry Park
Avanti Architects
Reimagined 2012

△ The 1,200-acre (485 hectare) former steel factory in central China has been abandoned for over a decade, made redundant through pollution levels and outdated technology.

The city of Chongqing, situated in a mountainous region of central China, grew as a critical military industrial base during China's long war with the Japanese from 1931–45. As Chinese hub cities like Shanghai, Changsha, and Wuhan fell to Japanese control many industrial factories relocated to Chongqing. In 1938 the Hanyang Iron and Steel Company moved its Wuhan headquarters to the city, rebranding itself the Chongqing Iron and Steelworks Company, and remained under state control until 1995. Due to worsening pollution output and increasingly outdated manufacturing equipment, the privatized company abandoned the 1,200-acre (485 hectare) facility in 2006, relocating its headquarters and leaving the vast site in disuse.

Public and private developers have focused on an ambitious redevelopment of the entire area. Chongqing Yufu Assets Management Group, a private developer with expertise in reclaimed abandoned factories, partnered with local government officials to set aside and transform sixty acres (twenty-four hectares) of the former steelworks facility into a new cultural attraction to celebrate local industrial history. Drawing

lessons from factory transformations in the UK and elsewhere around the world, and building upon a trend of rehabilitating and redeveloping the old industrial buildings in Chongqing, the group engaged Avanti Architects to reimagine the site after the firm won a 2012 design competition.

The Avanti team focused on ways to preserve the essential elements of the abandoned site, while updating spaces for its new future as a cultural attraction. One unique aspect of the former factory is the building layout, which was shaped by a linear production process, leading to long, large interior spaces. The master plan retains the north-south and east-west corridors as access points, leading to the central milling plant, the largest and oldest building on the site. Additional historic structures were to be maintained and refurbished, alongside features such as the factory's original brick chimneys and gasometer. Meeting and social spaces for the new museum were inspired by the original gathering spaces within the factory: the former company cafeteria will be transformed into a teahouse, and key hubs will be built near the locations of original bus shelters where factory workers would have

converged after a day's work. Meanwhile, a newly created "steel bar" building stretches across the site, allowing for coherent navigation that unifies the overall facility, and houses a bookstore, exhibition spaces, and museum ticketing facilities. Ten acres (four hectares) of the development are reserved for commercial or retail spaces, adjacent to the museum facility, reflecting an objective to further monetize the site.

As the pace of China's urbanization and real estate development has intensified, a new generation of designers and urbanists are seeking ways to preserve and celebrate Chinese history. The new museum in Chongqing, now a major urban area with over thirty million residents, will offer an opportunity to celebrate industrial heritage within the context of the former steelworks, using the abandoned building as a roadmap to its former use.

△ A vast site, the steelworks are now the subject of a major regeneration project that focuses on reuse of the large industrial remains.

▽ The raw cavernous interior has been reimagined as a new cultural attraction to celebrate local industrial history.

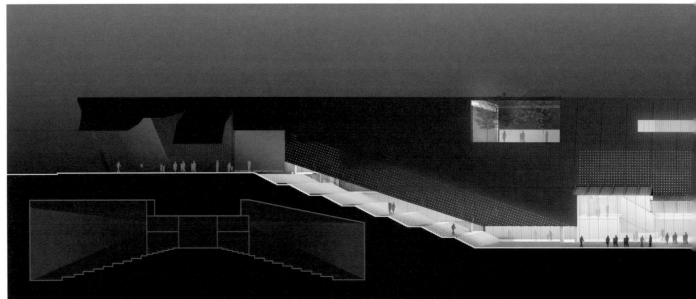

◁ The main milling plant is the largest building to be retained and would house the new industrial museum at the heart of the new quarter.

◁ A new cultural campus would replace the former industrial factory, retaining the essential shapes of original interiors while designing a welcoming venue for museum visitors.

▽ Alongside the museum, complementary uses include artists' workshops, bars, restaurants and retail spaces.

▽ Existing sheds of the former milling plant are rejuvenated and contrast with a new entrance building referred to as the "steel bar".

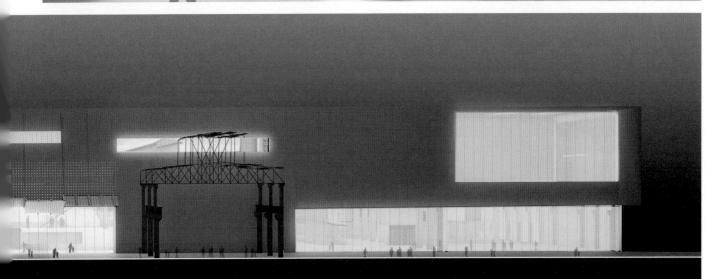

Zeitz Museum of
Contemporary Art Africa
Cape Town, South Africa
Heatherwick Studio

Gemini Residence
Copenhagen, Denmark
MVRDV

Gucci Hub
Milan, Italy
Piuarch

Museo Del Acero Horno[3]
Monterrey, Mexico
Grimshaw

Les Docks Cité de la Mode
et du Design
Paris, France
Jakob + MacFarlane

Fondazione Prada
Milan, Italy
OMA

Tate Modern
London, England
Herzog & de Meuron

La Fábrica
Sant Just Desvern, Spain
Ricardo Bofill

Gasometer City
Vienna, Austria
Jean Nouvel, Coop
Himmelb(l)au, Manfred
Wehdorn, Wilhelm
Holzbauer

Fooddock
Deventer, Netherlands
Wenink Holtkamp
Architecten

The Bentway
Toronto, Canada
City of Toronto,
Public Work, and teams

Alila Yangshuo Hotel
Guangxi, China
Vector Architects

Boekhandel Selexyz
Dominicanen
Maastricht, Netherlands
Merkx + Girod Architects

Zollverein Kohlenwäsche
Essen, Germany
OMA

High Line
New York, NY, USA
James Corner Field
Operations; Diller, Scofidio
and Renfro; Piet Oudolf

The Krane
Copenhagen, Denmark
Arcgency

Stony Island Arts Bank
Chicago, IL, USA
Theaster Gates

Gasholders London
London, England
Wilkinson Eyre

Bombay Sapphire Distillery
Hampshire, England
Heatherwick Studio

Forgotten

Transformed

What happens when an abandoned space is transformed into something else?

Creative projects—like producing a film, writing a book, or transforming an abandoned space are truly remarkable feats, given the many challenges and hurdles along the way. Architectural transformations require first and foremost a passion for preservation, followed by a definition of value; the commitment of significant design and strategy resources; the commitment of capital for construction; and the political and grassroots support to lead multi-stakeholder, multi-phase transformation processes. Throughout this effort, the project requires at least one consistent champion, willing to devote the necessary time, energy, and expertise to ensure both that the original structure remains intact and that the completed project follows through on its stated objectives of design and intended use.

The cases selected here have made it through each of these challenges, and have emerged on the other side of good ideas, shiny and new, an entirely different incarnation of the originally designed structures. They borrow the "bones" and "exoskeletons" of their former sites, but often go in vastly different directions in terms of form and function. These examples become models for designers and social entrepreneurs who may have fallen in love with an abandoned space and may have some inkling of an idea of a new life for it. They allow us not merely to marvel in the architectural accomplishments of these transformations, but also give us a chance to both study the process leading to their successful conversions and to assess their social impact and broader, longer-term outcomes within their communities. Good design, after all, is fundamentally concerned with how real people actually relate to a finished product.

As illustrated by the small sampling of successful transformation projects in this chapter, remnant spaces need not be particularly beautiful to inspire renovation. They certainly can be beautiful works of art that would typically be considered worthy of historical preservation, as we see in the cases of abandoned churches or elegantly designed banks. They can also be rather utilitarian, unconventional or even eyesores—from grain silos to factories, war bunkers, or dilapidated railways. What matters most at the outset is an indescribable, and perhaps entirely subjective, sense of magic and nostalgia. It is the emotional response, and not the logical one, that first animates the energy and passion for adaptive reuse. It is clear that buildings representing twentieth-century industrial and transportation infrastructure are currently inspiring a wide range of preservation and transformative designs. But this impulse to reimagine the magic and nostalgia of a forgotten space is as old as architecture itself. When one band of invaders conquered a new territory, it transformed old temples in its own image. So it goes today, even when developers would not consider themselves invaders.

After passing from the idea phase into real action, successful transformations then typically involve successful public-private partnerships, in which municipal, regional, or federal governments assume a leadership role in financing and/or incentivizing the redesign. In other words, nonprofit or for-profit leaders must partner with local communities and governments to actually acquire funding and get the thing built. The High Line in New York is among the best known examples of these kinds of alliances, in which a profound confluence of public and private interests allows dramatic redesigns to move ahead.

Once projects are viable financially, designers then must choose how much of the original structure—and the current state of the structure in all of its decayed, rusty charm—to retain, and how much to change. Purists or preservationists will argue for near-religious adherence to original form; Modernists might choose to drastically alter everything but the building site itself. Here, there are no clear rules. Like actors in a play, designers must choose how much attention they want from their audiences and how much their job is simply to retain the mood and character of the scene.

And then there is the final product, in which abandoned spaces assume a new kind of life. These projects range from the socially oriented, like community arts centers and public spaces, to primarily commercial endeavors, like hotels, fee-based tourist attractions, and high end residences. Here, of course, one sees the fruits of the design process itself. If local communities and neighborhoods, including the most vulnerable or excluded populations, are deeply and authentically engaged both as stakeholders and primary users from inception to opening, the completed designs will reflect a deeper and more authentic sense of social mission. When projects are built chiefly with commercial motives in mind, the final designs can be perceived as "spaceships landing in a desert" or "islands" with no authentic connection to surrounding neighborhoods, which alienate or even threaten longtime residents and businesses.

Ironically, in the end, transformed architecture and infrastructure, while ushering in a new season of hope for forgotten spaces, also spells true death for the ruins themselves. The very impulse to save and celebrate an abandoned site leads to its demise, not necessarily in the form of physical destruction but in the wholesale and final elimination of the original site's context. Brilliant as any design may be, no designer can bring back the past or restore old glories—despite what the glossy marketing brochures may tell you. It doesn't take an architect or an urban planner to reveal this. It is visceral. Newly reconfigured abandoned spaces, armed with real or superficial historical references, can foster a love of history and elevate a sense of place from the practical to the ethereal. They can also sell condominiums, attract tourists, or promote retail. At their most successful, they will still never compare to the magical experience of simply finding a forgotten site, covered in weeds and graffiti, in all its lonely grit and rebellious glamour. They can, however, make you dream of the past, and reimagine the future.

Grain Silo Complex
Cape Town, South Africa
Completed 1921
Abandoned 2001

Zeitz Museum of
Contemporary Art Africa
Heatherwick Studio
Transformed 2017

△ Along the waterfront in Cape Town, the original grain silo complex was the tallest building in sub-Saharan Africa.

Built in 1921 on the Victoria & Alfred Waterfront of Cape Town, the Grain Silo Complex instantly became the tallest building in the Southern Hemisphere and in sub-Saharan Africa. The silos were used to store and grade maize from the surrounding region, and remained an iconic feature on the city's skyline for decades, extending over 185 feet (56 meters) high.

The imposing complex comprised two main parts: a grading tower and forty-two 108 foot (33 meter) high concrete cylindrical tubes, each 18 feet (5.5 meters) in diameter. With the advent of containerized shipping, the complex was decommissioned in 2001. Yet its prime location on the Victoria & Alfred Waterfront, the most visited site in Africa, presented ample opportunities for transformation. Developers and owners in the local business district debated possible reuse for years, until a $38 million (R500 million) development plan was announced in 2013, one part of a master plan for the entire silo district.

Jochen Zeitz, a German businessman, art collector, and former CEO of Puma, worked with curator Mark Coetzee to turn his private collection into the first major museum dedicated to contemporary art from Africa and its diaspora. The London-based designer Thomas Heatherwick was engaged to design a museum of public civic significance, while preserving the site's historic shell.

Heatherwick's London studio designed a comprehensive rehabilitation of the entire structure of the silo complex, creating 100,000 square feet (9,300 square meters) across nine floors, with 65,000 square feet (6,000 square meters) dedicated to exhibition space. The top six floors of the fifteen-story building were transformed into a five-star hotel. The design objective for what Heatherwick described as "the world's tubiest building" was to give human dimension to the hulking concrete structure. To do so, the proposal carved out a central space of the tubular section for a social area, slicing through the cylindrical storage containers. Where the tubes were cut back, the edges reveal a contrast between the old material and the new laminate (inlaid in order to reinforce the structure).

The completed museum revolves around a huge atrium that spans the entire height of the tubes. Its shape is based on that of a single grain of maize—the product stored in the silos for so many years. This cathedral-sized atrium provides a network of gallery spaces within the tubular forms. To admit daylight, the carved-out tubes are capped by layers of laminated glass superimposed with fritted patterns commissioned from the late West African artist El Loko. This creates a glazed rooftop that is walkable and features a sculpture garden. The concrete walls of the grading tower are also cut away to create kaleidoscopic windows that allow natural daylight to generate a myriad of textures and colors throughout the interior.

The Zeitz Museum of Contemporary Art Africa (Zeitz MOCAA) opened in September 2017 and is the largest African art institution on the continent. It features one hundred galleries showcasing art created since 2000, along with spaces devoted to arts education, screenings, and performances. In both design and use, it reflects a powerful, stunning shift in the global narrative of African art.

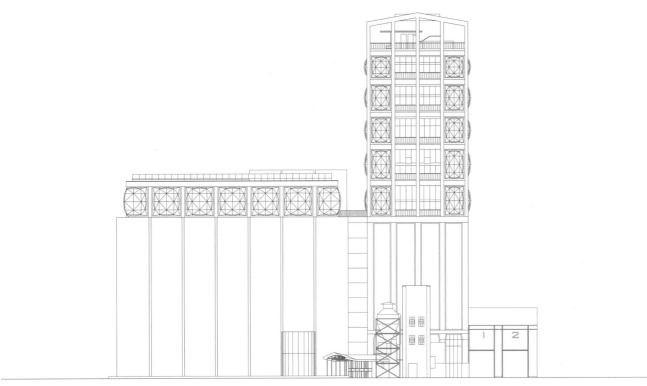

△ Elevation illustrating the complex's two main functions: a gallery and hotel above.

▽ Ground floor plan of the gallery, illustrating the central atrium void cut from tubes.

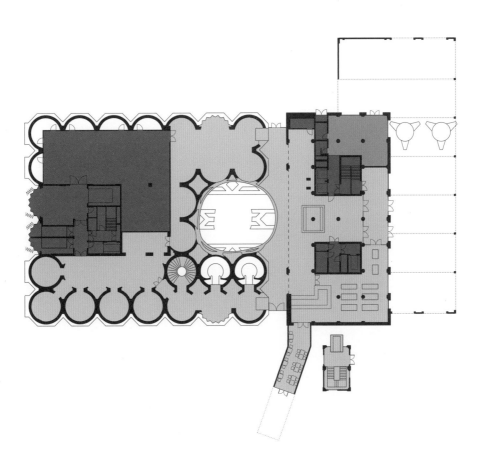

◁ △ The fifteen-story building is a comprehensive rehabilitation of the original grading tower and silo complex.

▷ At night, the building acts as a beacon in the harbor.

◁ The museum is planned around a huge atrium that spans the entire height of the tubes.

△ Concrete tubes, each 10 inches (250mm) thick, were carved away to create the interior.

▷ The cathedral-sized atrium provides a network of gallery spaces within the concrete tubes.

Dansk Soyakagefabrik
Copenhagen, Denmark
Completed 1909
Abandoned 1990s

Gemini Residence
MVRDV
Transformed 2005

△ The site of the demolished former soybean processing plant along Copenhagen's waterfront.

The Dansk Soyakagefabrik (Danish soybean cake factory) was built near the waterfront in Copenhagen's harbor district of Islands Brygge in 1909. By the 1950s, the company had become one of the largest local employers and, in 1963, two cylindrical concrete seed silos, known as Frøsilos, were constructed in order to meet the company's increasing production demands. The soybean-processing plant closed in the 1990s, a move that led to the abandonment of the entire facility for nearly two decades.

In the early 2000s the surrounding neighborhood began to be redeveloped into a new residential and commercial district. Given the desirability of the waterfront location, local developers focused on transforming the two eight-story silo towers into private residences. Architects Winy Maas, Jacob van Rijs, and Nathalie de Vries of the Rotterdam-based architectural practice MVRDV began the conversion of the seed silos— inspired by the potential of using their structures to achieve a futuristic effect, and of opening them up to embrace beautiful views along the waterfront.

Standing 138 feet (42 meters) high and 82 feet (25 meters) in diameter, the two silos were renovated in an interconnected manner, thus assuming the shape on plan of an infinity symbol in place of that of two distinct structures. The unstable structural integrity of the former silos required a delicate approach: windows could not simply be carved out of their exterior walls. To address this issue, the design team placed apartments directly on the building's exterior, which optimized natural daylight and balconies for each unit. The structures retained their original concrete cores for circulation and atria, reflecting their former industrial essence. Extending through their entire height, however, a new, transparent roof opened each one up to the sky and allowed natural sunlight to illuminate the interiors. In each of the resulting rotundas, austere white and black elements were added, conjuring up the atmosphere of an elegant spaceship. The white gallery parapets with their perforated steel panels were juxtaposed against black carpeting and insulated ceilings to control acoustics. No residential units were built on the ground floor, in an effort to offer a glimpse of the original atmosphere of the former silos.

The newly renovated Gemini Residence, named for the astrological zodiac sign connoting twins, officially opened in 2005. Its eighty-four apartments, curvilinear in shape, range in size from 970 to 2,200 square feet (90 to 200 square meters), and each allows for approximately 30 percent of additional outdoor balcony space with views overlooking the city. Whereas many residential conversions of abandoned industrial-infrastructure buildings tend toward the preservation of exteriors and the gutting of interiors, Gemini boldly transforms both the facade and the internal core of the former silo complex. At the same time, it manages to preserve the overall historical legacy of the buildings themselves. By "hanging" glass apartments around the exterior rather than filling the interior with residences, the project displays a bold, surprising new take on historical preservation and industrial reuse.

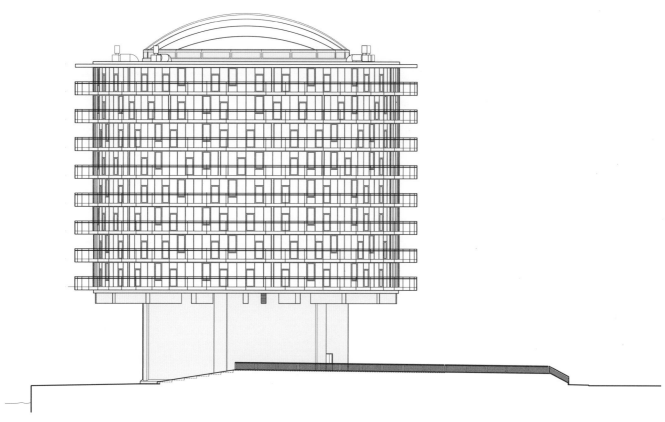

△ MVRDV reimagined the two eight-story towers into private residences, elevated above the original silo core.

▽ Concrete cores of the silos were structurally unstable, resulting in a design with apartments that wrapped the exterior.

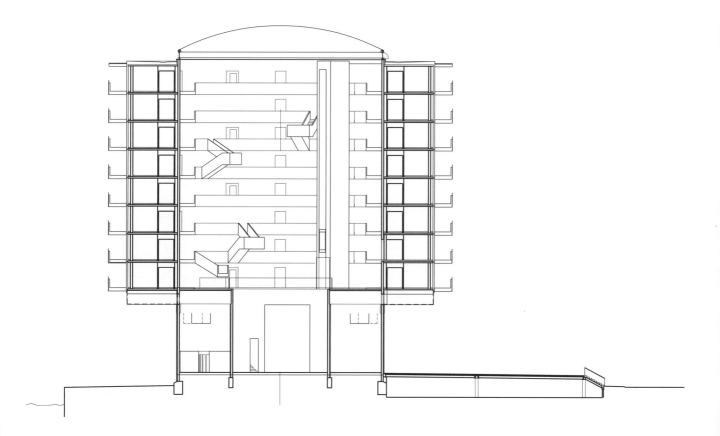

◁ A new, transparent roof over each of the silos opened the interiors to natural daylight. The illuminated inner cores now provide access and shared spaces for residents.

▽ ▷ In contrast with many residential conversions of abandoned industrial buildings, the design boldly transforms both the facade as well as the internal core of the silos.

△ Views from the residence units, unifying the building with the river and the city's skyline.

◁ By situating residences on the exterior and enclosing them in sheaths of glass, the new design optimizes exposure to the riverfront.

▷ The interior shell resembles the cool futuristic lines of a shapeship while retaining the cylindrical shape of the initial silos.

Caproni Factory
Milan, Italy
Completed 1915
Abandoned 1950

Gucci Hub
Piuarch
Transformed 2012

Δ For over thirty years, Caproni airplanes were constructed at a dedicated factory located just outside Milan.

In 1915, just east of Milan, a series of buildings was constructed to manufacture, test, and house aircraft designed by aviation pioneer Giovanni "Gianni" Battista Caproni. Hardly a bland warehouse-and-hangar complex, the factory buildings included elegant, brick structures alongside larger spaces. They evoked the spirit of a miniature, fully operational city, in which design, manufacture, and engineering functions coexisted. Bomber airplanes were manufactured on the 325,000 square foot (30,200 square meter) site throughout both world wars. In the postwar years, the dramatic decline in defense and military contracts prompted a similar decline in the Caproni business, leading to the factory's closure in 1950. Despite periodic reuse by artisans and as a warehouse, the site remained fundamentally unchanged for decades.

In the early 2000s the globally recognized fashion house Gucci sought a new international headquarters, and selected Milanese design firm Piuarch to repurpose the abandoned, iconic factory. Having worked on architectural projects for other leading fashion companies, the design team at Piuarch had long been enchanted with

the building; they focused on an approach that would retain the original architectural style while building a dynamic new kind of creative hub.

Structures built on the site in the 1960s, deemed by the Piuarch team to be incompatible with the historically significant buildings, were demolished. The facades of the original brick factory buildings were renovated but untouched, highlighting their gable-style shed roofs and allowing the site to retain the feeling of a "city." Large windows and glazed doors were added to increase the flow of natural light and link to the outdoors. The hangar was repurposed into a flexible open space, to be transformed twice annually for Gucci's fashion-week presentations, and was connected to an outdoor pedestrian square. A new six-story office tower was built adjacent to these structures, with exposed steel framing on glass exteriors, in an effort to unify the new building with the originals. Tree planting, plazas, gardens, and a pedestrian path built in place of the former factory's driveway instilled a more communal sensiblity and a closer connection to nature for the 322,900 square foot (30,000 square meter) project. Energy-efficient

measures of Piuarch's redesign included installing photovoltaic and geothermal energy sources, reducing water usage by an estimated 20 percent and energy costs by 25 percent. During the process of renovating the buildings, over 90 percent of waste products were recycled.

Drawing inspiration from the simple beauty and modular flexibility of the original factory, the new Gucci headquarters opened in 2012—a multipurpose space comprising showrooms, a canteen, a restaurant, photo studios, graphic design facilities, indoor-and-outdoor pedestrian spaces, and open space for runway fashion shows. Gucci creative director Alessandro Michele designed the interiors, splashing various spaces with bold colors and patterns. By displaying reverence for the former factory's past while explicitly adding modern flourishes and literally opening the space to the fashion world, the Gucci Hub opens a new chapter for both the charming buildings and for an Italian legacy of ingenuity, engineering, and design.

△ The factory structures included elegant brick halls with sawtooth glazing.

▽ The large site was purpose-built and delivered bomber airplanes for both world wars.

△ The airplane factory was like a miniature, operational city for design, manufacture, and engineering.

▽ Despite brief occupations by artists and squatters while vacant, the factory's fundamental design remained untouched.

△ A dramatic decline in defense and military
contracts saw a similar decline for Caproni.

▽ The factory was eventually closed in 1950
and remained unused for more than fifty years.

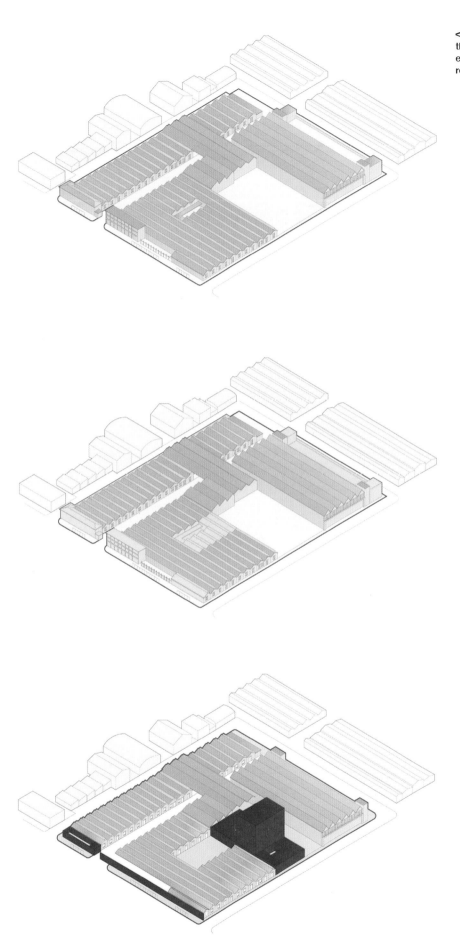

◁ Schematic drawing showing evolution of the design: original abandoned factory; 1960s expansion removed from the site (yellow); final reimagined Gucci complex (blue).

∇ A new six-story tower is used for corporate offices, while the repurposed hangar and brick buildings constitute an integrated campus.

◁ Facades of the original brick factory buildings were renovated but untouched, highlighting their gable-style shed roofs.

▽ The complex is knitted together by pedestrian routes that run between all buildings, creating landscaped and open spaces.

▷ Faithful to the original architecture, the renovation includes the large hangar, which now hosts events and fashion shows.

▷ Large windows and glazed doors were added to increase the flow of natural light and link to the outdoors, respecting the modularity of the original buildings.

Compañia Fundidora de Fierro y Acero
Monterrey, Mexico
Arthur G. McKee & Co.
Completed 1900–1966
Abandoned 1986

Museo Del Acero Horno³
Grimshaw
Transformed 2007

Δ   A leading steel producer in Mexico, the Monterrey foundry featured a 230 foot (70 meter) blast furnace, Horno Alto #3.

A steel production facility in Monterrey, Mexico, originally built by the Compañia Fundidora de Fierro y Acero in 1900, would become one of the most prolific steel foundries in the world and an important aspect of the city's local identity. Producing iron and steel for major infrastructure development countrywide, for decades the foundry was also of paramount importance for Monterrey's economic and social sustainability. In the 1960s, a new 230 foot (70 meter) blast furnace, Horno Alto #3, was built to accommodate increased demand and growth in the steel industry. Designed by U.S. engineering firm Arthur G. McKee & Co., it was the first automated blast furnace in Mexico, allowing for a dramatic increase in steel production. It continued to be used until 1986, when it was decommissioned as the company fell into bankruptcy due to increasing global competition.

After lying abandoned for two years, in 1988 the federal government granted the state government permission to turn the entire Monterrey Foundry site into a public park that would reflect the cultural and economic history of the former industrial complex. The Parque Fundidora repurposed several industrial structures, added an artificial lake and paths for walking and cycling, and built tourist attractions like a hotel, children's park, entertainment venues, and a convention center. As a National Industrial Archaeological Heritage Site and covering 350 acres (142 hectares) of land, the park would come to attract roughly two million visitors every year. Despite its growth, however, Horno Alto #3 remained abandoned for twenty years.

In 2005, the architectural firm Grimshaw was selected to design a new museum in and around the iconic decommissioned furnace, to be called Museo Del Acero Horno³—the Museum of Steel. The team endeavored to honor the historic spirit of the structure while pushing the boundaries of the use of steel in fabrication and design, adding elements like a tessellated, steel-plate roof and a helical staircase. The museum reuses the interior of the furnace itself, featuring a colorful, pyrotechnic "Furnace Show" to bring steelmaking history to life for visitors in the former Cast Hall, while additional rooms were transformed into a café and offices. The building's exterior was left largely untouched, with light sandblasting and protective coatings applied to leave an enduring patina. The original iron ore elevator features a salvaged cable car elevator, transporting passengers 140 feet (43 meters) to a labyrinth of exterior walkways circling the facility and offering stunning views of the city, the adjacent mountains, and into the furnace itself. A new wing was built for additional gallery space and museum facilities, which have green roofs featuring native grasses and which harvest rainwater, allowing for both plant irrigation and storm mitigation.

Completed in 2007 and opened to coincide with the city's hosting of the Universal Forum of Cultures, Museo Del Acero Horno³ adds 9,000 square feet (836 square meters) of new exhibition, museum, and educational space to the surrounding park. The transformation of the former furnace mirrors the changing dynamic of Monterrey: once a global leader in steel production, the city has entered a new century focused on new technologies and innovative design.

△ Abandoned in 1986, the Mexican government proceeded to transform the surrounding areas into a national public park.

▽ Cross section of the building illustrating its transformation into a new museum with a central re-created blast furnace.

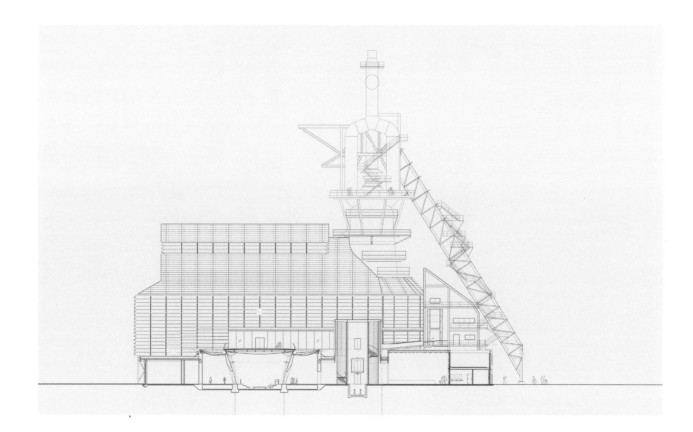

△ ▷ To respect the history and form of the existing structure, the museum's renovation included a sympathetic new envelope, which mirrors the original foundry.

◁ Offering a light touch, the new addition to the museum included a partially sunken steel gallery, housed in the former slag heap.

△ A catwalk at the apex of the steelworks gives visitors far-reaching views to Monterrey and the distant Sierra Madre.

▷ To act as a showcase for contemporary uses of steel, a dramatic sweeping helical steel staircase links the lower floors.

▷ Interiors retain the original burnished steel and brick of the foundry.

Les Docks Magasins
Paris, France
Georges Morin-Goustiaux
Completed 1907
Abandoned 1984

Les Docks Cité de la Mode et du Design
Jakob + MacFarlane
Transformed 2009

△ An early image of the Parisian industrial warehouses along the River Seine.

In order to create an industrial warehouse for the bustling river trade of the early twentieth-century Parisian economy, the Port of Paris commissioned a design from architect Georges Morin-Goustiaux in 1907. The completed structure, which enabled the Magasins Généraux to store goods along the River Seine en route to the Gare d'Austerlitz rail terminus, has been described as perhaps the first modern dock development of the twentieth century. Among the first reinforced concrete structures in the French capital, it abstained from adopting an elegant, decorative facade. This aesthetic decision was a source of controversy at the time, with some critics perceiving an eyesore and others marveling at the resulting building's modern, utilitarian sensibility.

Throughout the twentieth century, the warehouse became less essential for merchandise shipping and storage, and by the 1980s the space was used primarily as a carpet warehouse and examination facility. In 2004 the City of Paris held a design competition to reinvigorate the site as part of a neighborhood development strategy, and left it up to the discretion of proposing design teams to determine whether to retain or demolish

the existing Morin-Goustiaux structure. The selected design team, Parisian architects Jakob + MacFarlane, opted to retain the remnant skeleton of the former warehouse while envisioning a vibrant new facade for the abandoned building.

Jakob + MacFarlane's design called for a refurbishment of the initial concrete structure, but replaced the exterior with a green "plug-over" concept inspired by the movements of the Seine. Green, faceted glass would protrude from the building, lending an iconic exterior to a faceless structure and evoking comparisons with caterpillars, snakes, and twisting vines. The green color balances the natural reflections of the water in the river below, and at night offers a unique glow, due to the additions of lighting artist Yann Kersalé. The overall effect draws the viewer into a fascinating interplay of nature and technology, with the "skin" of the new glass structure enveloping the historic site like fresh branches on an old tree.

Les Docks Cité de la Mode et du Design (The Dock City of Fashion and Design) opened to the public in 2009, bringing new style to Paris' 13th Arrondissement and attracting nearly 1.5 million

visitors per year. It truly was envisioned as a "city within a city," featuring a multifaceted venue of 160,000 square feet (15,000 square meters). Weaving through the site are the prestigious Institut Français de la Mode (French Institute of Fashion); a contemporary art museum, Art Ludique; and multiple shops, bookstores, and restaurants.

Today, one of Paris' top cultural attractions and an important center for French fashion and style, the renovated docks have become a beloved and quirky landmark along the city's waterfront. With a surprising mixture of historical preservation and innovative design, Les Docks Cité have managed to breathe new life into its surrounding neighborhood, with a rebellious spirit that invites Parisians to reclaim this site as a new center for creativity.

△ By the 1980s the original warehouses for the
Magasins Généraux had fallen into disuse.

▽ The architects proposed stretching an undu-
lating skin over the concrete bones of the docks.

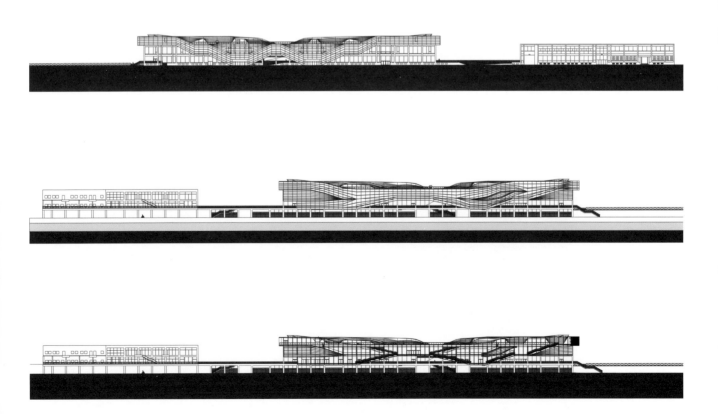

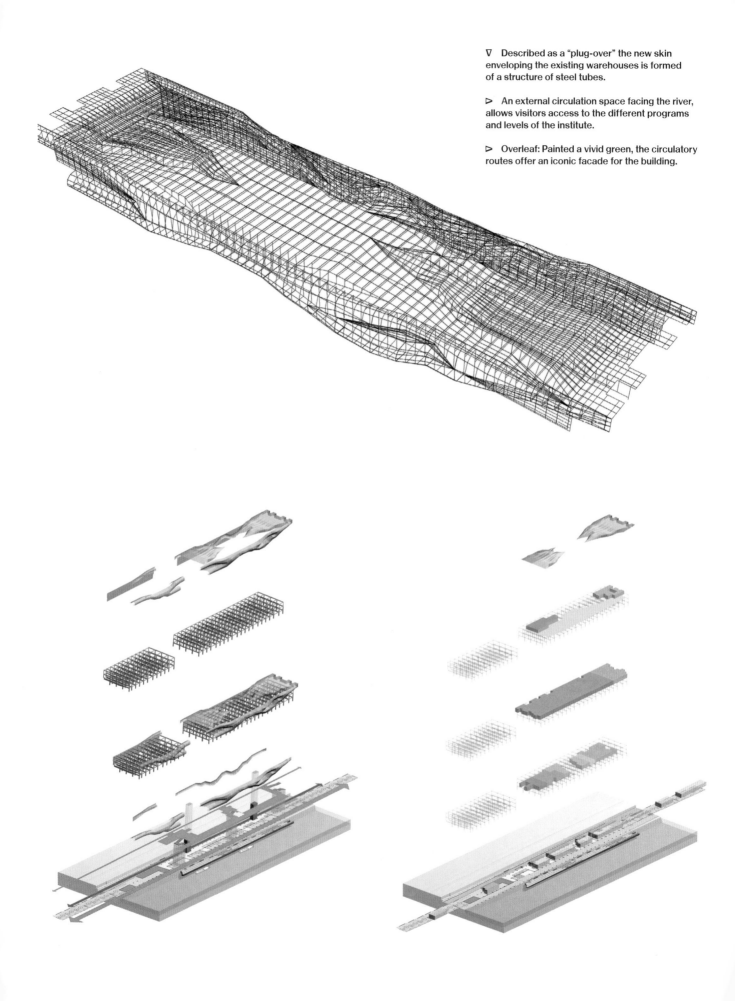

▽ Described as a "plug-over" the new skin enveloping the existing warehouses is formed of a structure of steel tubes.

▷ An external circulation space facing the river, allows visitors access to the different programs and levels of the institute.

▷ Overleaf: Painted a vivid green, the circulatory routes offer an iconic facade for the building.

Gin Distillery
Milan, Italy
Completed 1910
Abandoned Unknown

Fondazione Prada
OMA
Transformed 2015

△ For its new art center, the Fondazione Prada selected an abandoned former gin distillery on the outskirts of Milan.

A gin distillery was built in the 1910s on Largo Isarco in the industrial zone of Vigentino, south of the center of Milan, but later abandoned. Though left in disrepair, the original warehouses, silos, and laboratories remained on the site, which lay adjacent to a train station and offered a unique set of contrasting scales and spaces. Inspired by the rawness of the site and its location on the outskirts of Italy's fashion capital, Fondazione Prada determined to transform the area into an arts center.

To re-envision the space, Miuccia Prada and Patrizio Bertelli, the cofounders of Fondazione Prada, turned to longtime collaborator Rem Koolhaas of OMA and his firm's research arm, AMO. The Fondazione—focused as it was on moving beyond the realm of fashion, and dedicated to art, film, philosophy, and other disciplines—had been holding contemporary art exhibitions in abandoned warehouses and churches since 1995. Recognizing both a need to permanently house the couple's art collection and also to fill a void from lack of public support for cultural institutions across Europe, the Fondazione purchased the land and funded the entire project.

Koolhaas' design creates a diversity of spaces for presenting art in a variety of media. A nondescript building, nicknamed the "Haunted House" by Miuccia Prada herself, was dramatically transformed by encrusting it in 24-karat gold leaf, leaving only the glass of its windows exposed. The reflective gold material offers a glittering counterbalance to the gray landscape of adjacent historic buildings and the Milanese skyline. The luxurious color stands as an iconic beacon of the renewed space, despite its relatively inexpensive material cost. The exteriors of other buildings are left largely untouched while yet others are reconfigured to merely appear untouched, balancing the introduction of new materials of glass, concrete, and aluminum.

OMA created three new structures on the campus, which encompasses 120,000 square feet (11,100 square meters) of exhibition space: a two-level gallery space, the Podium, and a multifunctional auditorium, the Cinema, both of which opened in 2015, and a new nine-story tower building, the Torre, completed in 2018. Bar Luce, a candy-colored café designed by filmmaker Wes Anderson, offers references to Milan's

nineteenth-century shopping arcade, the Galleria Vittorio Emanuele, and manages to cultivate an environment that allows visitors to feel as if they are part of a movie set.

Notably, there is not a Prada backpack or a couture item for sale—a conscious decision by the Fondazione cofounders to downplay any corporate branding and commerciality that might have tempted others. The complex therefore manages to focus entirely on the display of ideas and creative expression, without explicit traces of the venerable fashion house behind it. The space hums with an unshakable spirit of utilitarian beauty—much like Milan itself, much like the original distillery buildings, and the designers behind it. While Milan has long been recognized as an international center for fashion and furniture design, the introduction of the Fondazione Prada has now created a global destination for contemporary art as well.

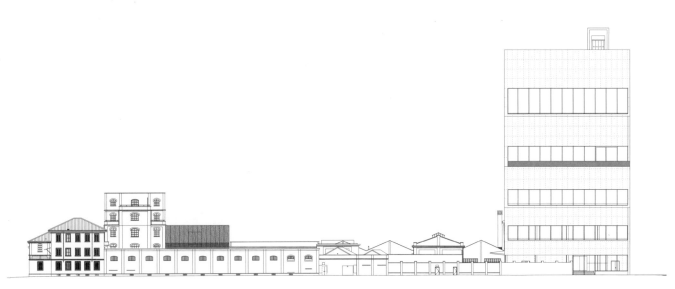

△ The design by OMA features reuse of the existing gin factory structures along with three new buildings.

∇ The western extent of the site is marked by a nine-story tower of gallery spaces, the Torre.

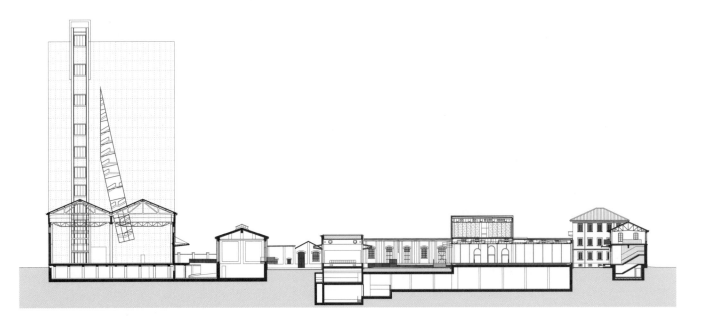

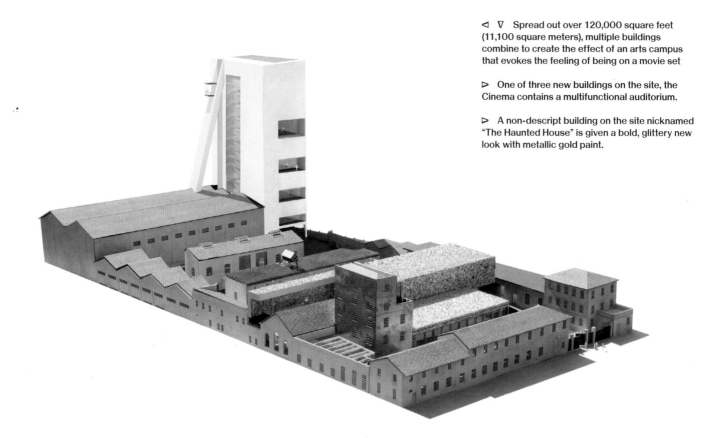

◁ ▽ Spread out over 120,000 square feet (11,100 square meters), multiple buildings combine to create the effect of an arts campus that evokes the feeling of being on a movie set

▷ One of three new buildings on the site, the Cinema contains a multifunctional auditorium.

▷ A non-descript building on the site nicknamed "The Haunted House" is given a bold, glittery new look with metallic gold paint.

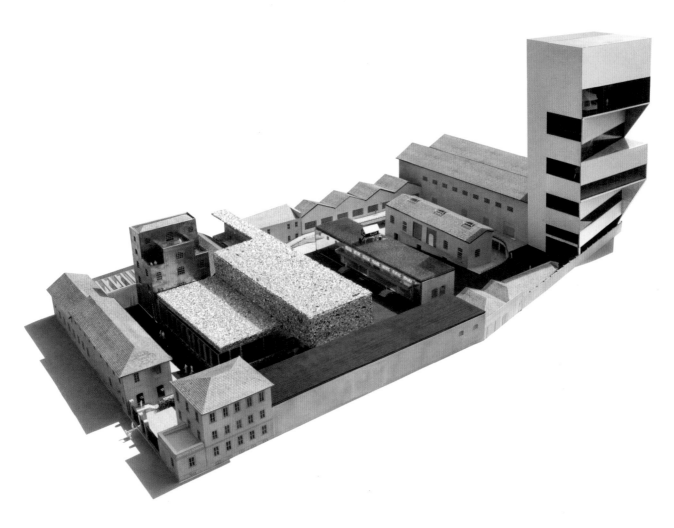

◁ ▽ By retaining the shape and placement of existing structures, the complex offers a sense of a small village, with passageways connecting buildings to each other.

▷ The alluring gold facade offers a visual counterbalance to the muted tones elsewhere, imbuing the overall site with a memorable appearance.

▷ Overleaf: The art complex has become an instant classic in the Italian fashion capital, delivering art and design far from Milan's city center.

Bankside Power Station
London, England
Sir Giles Gilbert Scott
Completed 1963
Abandoned 1981

Tate Modern
Herzog & de Meuron
Transformed 2000

Δ   The Bankside Power Station cut a regal, imposing position on London's riverfront, earning the nickname, "cathedral of power".

Originally built in 1891 to supply electricity to the City of London, Bankside was designated during World War II to become London's only oil-powered electricity power station. City officials commissioned the designer Sir Giles Gilbert Scott, who was then well known for having designed iconic London structures such as Battersea Power Station, Waterloo Bridge, and the red British telephone booth. Opening in 1963, the new Bankside station was envisaged as a "cathedral of power," underscoring the vaunted role of electrical power in twentieth-century urban society and architecture. It was vast and imposing, with a central chimney nearly 325 feet (100 meters) tall and its main bulk extending 650 feet (200 meters) long with a grand turbine hall at its core, a boiler house to the north, and a switch house to the south. Public discomfort relating to its proximity to St. Paul's Cathedral—which sat just opposite, across the River Thames—led to requirements that the power station be 50 feet (15 meters) shorter in height than the cathedral.

Decommissioned as an electricity generation facility in 1981, Bankside fell out of use for over a decade. The surrounding Southwark neighborhood

continued its decline, with a postindustrial sense of dilapidation throughout the 1980s. Acquired by the Tate Gallery in 1994, a design competition led to the selection of Herzog & de Meuron for its repurposing into a gallery of modern art.

Inspired by both cost constraints and its awe-inspiring scale, the redesign included retention of the core original structure and few grand alterations. Stripping the building back to its bare steel-and-brick frame, the huge machinery and roof of the main turbine hall, together with the roof of the old boiler house were removed, allowing the previously dark power station to be drenched in natural light. The main turbine hall was gutted for installations, while the building's separate parts house galleries of varying sizes. The two-story, glass extension on one half of the roof and the rooftop "light beam" bring twenty-first-century modernity to the brick structure, enhancing and lightening the behemoth rather than radically adapting it. The turbine hall becomes a main plaza to the unpretentious exhibition spaces, where no gallery is privileged over any other. A long ramp in the entrance hall adds an ethereal effect, both inviting

visitors into a grand plaza and reminding them of the scale of the building.

After opening in 2000, Tate Modern welcomed 5.25 million visitors in its first year—immediately doubling the foot traffic of all three existing Tate galleries combined (the original "Tate Britain", and outposts in Liverpool and St Ives). This overwhelming popularity led to an expansion into the Tanks and the Switch House in 2016—again, redesigned with a light touch by Herzog & de Meuron—allowing for a diverse array of exhibition, installation, and event venues.

Today Tate Modern is one of the largest and most visited modern art galleries in the world, and has led to a dramatic transformation of Southwark as a cultural destination. It represents the quintessential transformation of the postindustrial age: a "cathedral of power" becoming a "cathedral for modern art."

△ The power facility was decommissioned in
1981, and the surrounding neighborhood experienced postindustrial decline.

▽ The vast scale of the Turbine Hall attracted
the Tate Gallery and was entirely reinterpreted
to become a "cultural cathedral".

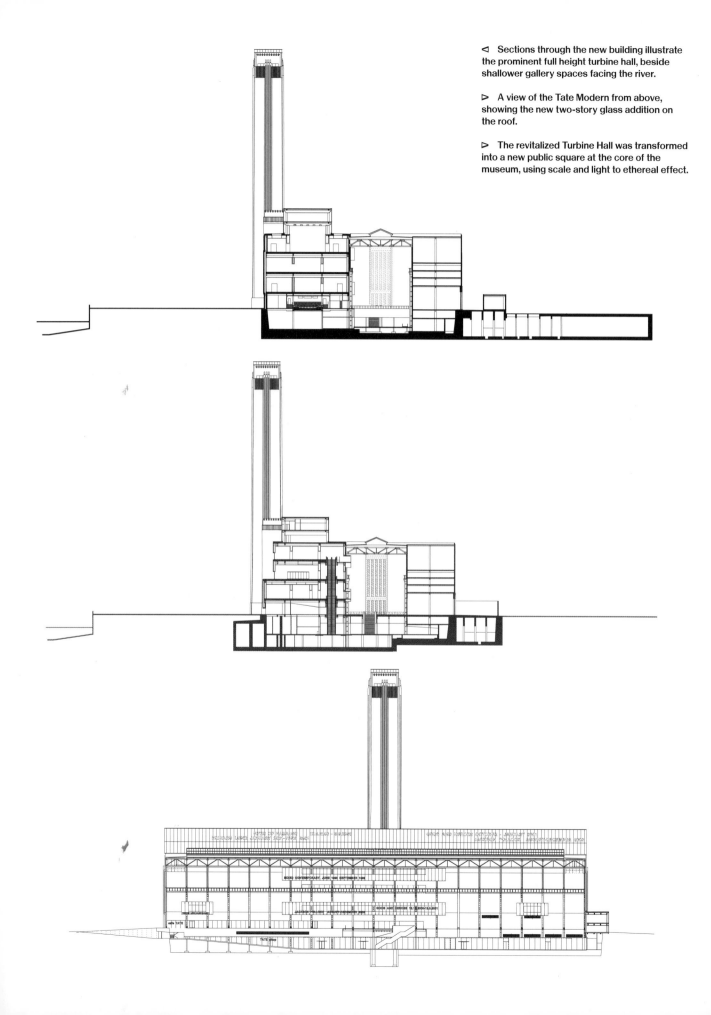

◁ Sections through the new building illustrate the prominent full height turbine hall, beside shallower gallery spaces facing the river.

▷ A view of the Tate Modern from above, showing the new two-story glass addition on the roof.

▷ The revitalized Turbine Hall was transformed into a new public square at the core of the museum, using scale and light to ethereal effect.

△ In the central turbine hall, the design retains the raw industrial scale and materials, creating a gallery that was the first of its kind globally.

▷ The juxtaposition of old and new provides a contemplative setting for the introduction of modern art installations.

Cement factory
Sant Just Desvern, Spain
Completed 1921
Abandoned 1968

La Fábrica
Ricardo Bofill
Transformed 1975–

△ An aerial view showing the extent of the
abandoned World War I cement factory and
its surroundings.

On the outskirts of Barcelona a giant cement factory was constructed during the first phase of World War I–era industrialization in Catalonia. It was gradually built over time, gaining various additions as different chains of production became necessary within the factory. The facility comprised over thirty silos, two and a half miles (four kilometers) of underground tunnels, and huge engine rooms—all of which lay in partial states of ruin after its abandonment. The successive layers of design were made visible through the varied aesthetic language of the buildings. Once-purposeful staircases now led, paradoxically, to nowhere; industrial elements hung, absurdly, over open voids; huge spaces were useless without their former industrial purpose, yet charmingly odd in their proportions. A brutal functionality came across in the building materials: sculptural in quality but abruptly treated. By the 1970s, the complex had become known to locals primarily as an eyesore and a source of pollution.

Yet, as a young architect in 1973, Ricardo Bofill fell in love with the factory. He resolved to purchase the site and its surrounding grounds, and gradually transform it into a dreamlike labyrinth of gardens, workplaces, and his own family residence. Attracted by the contradictory elements of the space, he decided to retain the factory and modify the stark aspects and aesthetic disjuncture of the building, assigning new functions to its industrial forms. After demolishing over two thirds of the structures on the site, Bofill worked with Catalan craftsmen for over a year and a half to preserve the rest. Dynamite and jackhammers were required to alter the concrete-filled structures, rendered almost impenetrable after decades of concrete dust sitting stagnant on them. The structures were "greened," with plants that would eventually climb the concrete walls and hang high off the siloed roofs.

Bofill installed various forms from the history of architecture, giving the former cement factory the appearance of a modern castle. Today, the design is widely recognized as a masterpiece of postmodern architecture. The former silo area became a studio space for his architecture firm, Ricardo Bofill Taller de Arquitectura, while the underground galleries were transformed into archive and model-workshop spaces. The factory hall was converted into a conference and exhibition space with ceilings thirty-two feet (ten meters) high, nicknamed the Cathedral, or *La Catedral*. The residence transforms brute, cubic, concrete space by adding arched windows. Throughout the factory, oxidized concrete stays true to the original industrialism. The exterior of the buildings open onto lush green gardens, which feature olive trees, eucalyptus, and cypress. Mischievous vines wander from building to building, playing with the site's abandoned past and producing an enchanting dialogue between nature and industry.

Today Bofill works and lives in a 5,382 square foot (500 square meter) portion of La Fábrica (The Factory), and has claimed that here his personal and professional lives blend seamlessly. By fusing his design work and his personal family space, the building becomes a monument to both the art of living and the passion of one's practice—a living, breathing factory of a different kind.

△ The site's dilapidated buildings included whimsical silos, tunnels, lyrical staircases, and broad open spaces.

▽ Early sketches by Ricardo Bofill illustrate the transformation of the factory into a mixed use project that recalls a modern castle.

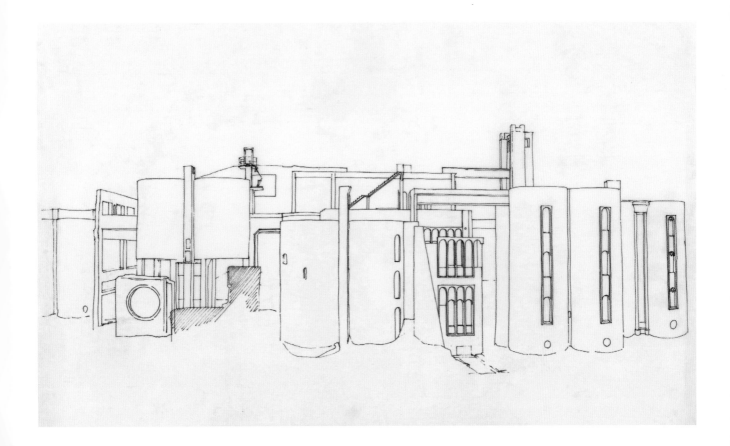

△ ▷ The reinvigorated designs turn the ruin
into a fortress, in which invasive greenery is duly
invited to carpet the buildings.

◁ Brute cubic concrete volumes are softened by the addition of arched doors and windows.

∇ The redesigned interiors provide a dramatic
backdrop for public events, contemplative study,
and reverence for the remnant structures.

△ A portion of the former factory was reimagined and now provides living quarters for Bofill and his family.

▷ Places to study and meet make careful use of the unique compositions of light, space, and pre-existing materials.

Gaswerk Simmering
Vienna, Austria
Schimming
Completed 1899
Abandoned 1986

Gasometer City
Jean Nouvel, Coop Himmelb(l)au, Manfred Wehdorn, Wilhelm Holzbauer
Transformed 2001

△ Gas storage facilities in Vienna were built in 1899 in the form of four giant iconic cylinders, known as gasometers.

In 1892 the city of Vienna held an international competition for the design of gas storage facilities that could keep pace with the energy demands of the vibrant capital. Between 1896 and 1899, the Gaswerk was built by a German engineer named Schimming in the industrial Simmering neighborhood to supply gas to Vienna's street lamps and households. Composed of four giant cylindrical containers known as gasometers, each massive tank could hold over 3 million cubic feet (85,000 cubic meters) of gas, was built with brick exteriors topped by glass domes, and extended 230 feet (70 meters) high and 200 feet (60 meters) in diameter.

Gaswerk Simmering served its purpose for over eight decades, but as gas storage increasingly moved to underground facilities the functional need for the gasometers decreased. Yet their industrial beauty captivated the interest of city leaders. In 1978 they were designated protected landmarks. After being entirely abandoned by 1986, the large, circular structures were used as a popular site for rave dance parties due to their ability to generate powerful

echoes, and even as the stark setting of a James Bond film.

By the 1990s local architect and preservationist Manfred Wehdorn had begun advocating the repurposing of the grand structures. In 1995 the City of Vienna staged another architecture competition, and chose designs from four leading architects for each of the four structures: Jean Nouvel for Gasometer A, Coop Himmelb(l)au for Gasometer B, Manfred Wehdorn himself for Gasometer C, and Wilhelm Holzbauer for Gasometer D.

Each given their own tank to redesign, the architects turned the interiors of the four storage facilities into modern apartments and commercial spaces while preserving their exterior brick facades. Jean Nouvel's repurposed Gasometer A includes a spacious indoor plaza, highlighting the interplay of light and shadow from its large, web-like overhead windows. For Gasometer B, Coop Himmelb(l)au built a twenty-two-story, bending structure to attach to the drum, which itself features a soundproof event hall. Manfred Wehdorn, in designing the interior of Gasometer C, focused on the implementation of lush, green

gardens; terraced balconies for residences; and a courtyard atrium to provide natural light to the lower level. Wilhelm Holzbauer designed Gasometer D with a strong focus on fostering a greater sense of community, containing a central cluster of residential blocks.

Taken together the four newly designed structures compose a new civic concept, known collectively as "Gasometer City". By juxtaposing residential apartments, office space, retail space, media venues, and even the Vienna City and County Archives, it can be viewed as a veritable city within a city. Over one thousand people reside in its six hundred residences, and a new U-Bahn subway station was built to connect Gasometer City to central Vienna. More than a megaproject, it fosters a genuine sense of community where people live, work, and spend leisure time. It is a unique showcase of cooperation among architects, and a leading example of an effort to reclaim abandoned energy infrastructure for social use in the modern era.

△ Acquiring landmark protection as gas storage moved underground, the massive structures presented a unique redesign opportunity.

▽ Restored and reused, the intricate brick facades and elaborate window designs are integral to the Gasometer City buildings.

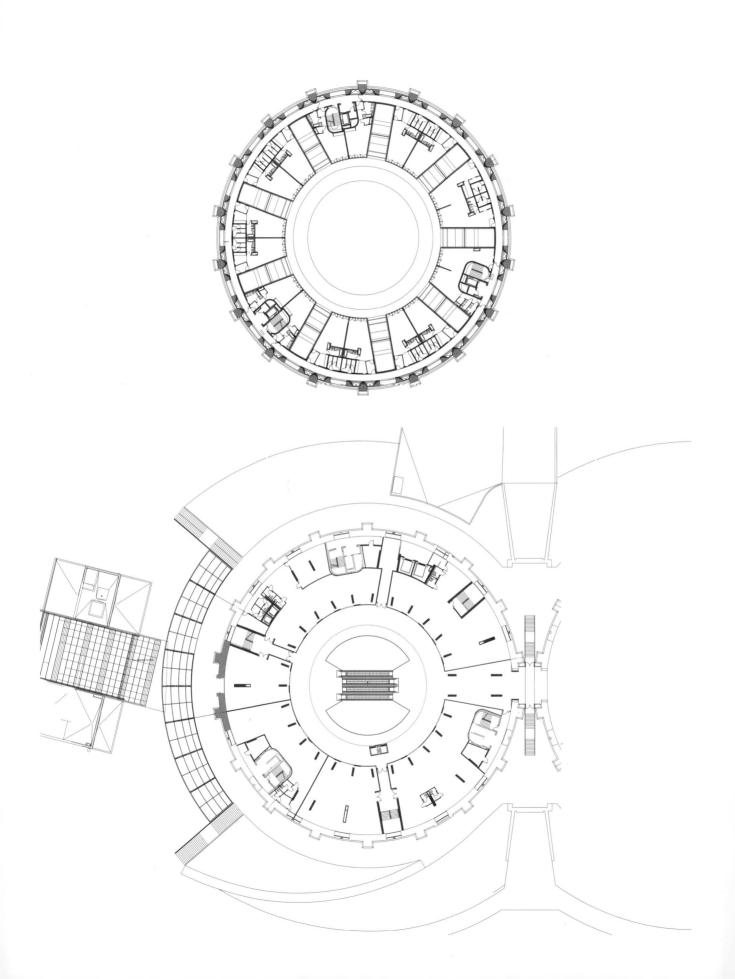

◁ Floor plans of Jean Nouvel's gasometer design illustrate the radial arrangement of apartments, set around a central open core, devised to create spaces in harmony with the existing circular structures.

▽ The heavily articulated exteriors of the gasometers reflect a general preference when they were built to disguise industrial buildings, despite their expanse and 236-foot (72-meter) height.

◁ The four gasometers are united by their preserved walls of brick, and linked by a retail complex that runs through the lowest level.

▽ ▷ In contrast with the solid, brick exteriors, the interior glazed cladding of Jean Nouvel's design is arranged in segments, which creates reflections and a perceived sense of lightness.

De Zwarte Silo
Deventer, Netherlands
Maarten van Harte,
A. J. Lammers
Completed 1923
Abandoned 1990

Fooddock
Wenink Holtkamp
Architecten
Transformed 2015

△ The grain storage silo in the Dutch city
of Deventer served as part of a critical trade
shipment route for much of the twentieth century.

Along the harbor in Deventer, one of the oldest cities in the Netherlands, a series of storage silos was built by the A.J. Lammers Company in 1923. It included a tall silo for the storage of grain; a lower building for storing salt; and additional buildings to be used as stables, warehouses, and offices—all for food processing and production. Designed by local architect Maarten van Harte, the tallest concrete silo was built to hold 1,500 tons of grain. After several years of use, however, moisture began to seep into the silo during heavy rainfalls, until eventually a coat of bitumen was applied to waterproof the structure's exterior. This led to its noteworthy black color, which resulted in it becoming known as the Zwarte Silo, or Black Silo. A symbol of the twentieth-century transformation of the harbor, it was used for decades as an active silo along trade shipment routes until it was abandoned in 1990.

After lying in a state of disuse until 2010, the site drew the interest of BOEi, a local civic organization, which imagined transforming the site into a community amenity. Dutch architects Wenink Holtkamp were commissioned to reinterpret the former grain silo as a new food hall while retaining the architectural integrity of the space itself. The silo had an insular, sober character, but the designers sought to open up the space to the adjacent port, to give it greater appeal to local residents and contribute to enlivening the harbor.

Within the silo itself, the design team retained and preserved the majority of its original elements in raw form—including thirty loading cells, ducts, pipes, silo cones, and concrete walls and pillars—in order to preserve the historical feeling of the space. Meanwhile, the addition of a new forty-foot (twelve-meter) opening was built to fill the space with light, orient it toward the waterfront, and to create an inviting and airy environment. The team also redeveloped the two lower brick buildings on the site, transforming one space into additional food stalls and a bar while the other main area was converted into a flexible event venue. The restoration of large, steel-framed windows and doors and the addition of sizable skylights in the event venue flood these spaces with light as well. Various shades of gray, particularly steel gray, help to unify the interiors, accentuating a feeling of industrial rawness.

With redesign completed in 2015, the Zwarte Silo reopened as Fooddock, a collection of food trucks and stalls from a diverse range of gastronomic entrepreneurs. Fresh produce and prepared provisions are available within the food hall, underscoring a link to the silo's historic use as a key stop along the spectrum of food production and consumption. Alongside the event venue, the redevelopment has become part of a larger narrative involving the reclamation of disused industrial structures in the area, imbuing forgotten spaces with a new vitality and public spirit.

△ ▽ To maintain the raw history of the building, the new adaptation purposely retained elements integral to its previous use, such as hoppers, distribution chutes, and disused equipment.

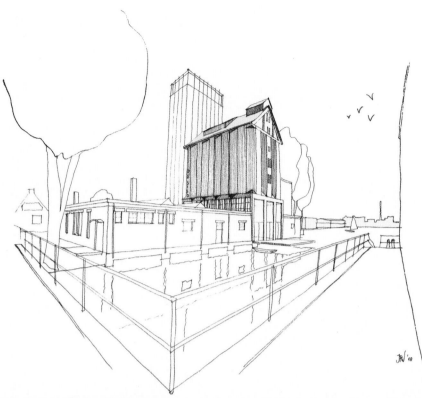

◁   In keeping with the building's nickname "Black Silo" this schematic drawing for its transformation by Wenink Holtkamp Architecten retains the prominent black skin of the old silo structure.

▽   ▷   The Zwarte Silo complex was transformed into a public food hall, opening the building and the site towards the river and the surrounding waterfront.

▷   Overleaf: The redevelopment has become part of a larger narrative involving the reclamation of disused industrial structures in the area.

Gardiner Expressway
Toronto, Canada
City of Toronto
Completed 1966
Abandoned 1990s

The Bentway
City of Toronto,
Public Work, and teams
Transformed 2016

△ Dividing Toronto's residential city and industrial waterfront, the Gardiner Expressway extended eleven miles (eighteen kilometers).

1

The Gardiner Expressway was built in the 1960s in Toronto to meet car-traffic demands in the rapidly expanding city. The expressway extended eleven miles (eighteen kilometers), partly running alongside Lake Ontario, with elevated and at-grade sections weaving their way through multiple city neighborhoods. Initial construction necessitated the demolition of homes and existing parklands. By the 1990s the expressway had begun deteriorating in multiple locations, especially its elevated sections, due to the extensive use of road salt in winter. Despite some remedial work in the 1990s, an elevated segment was demolished in 2001 and various proposals to dismantle or replace remaining elevated portions were considered, as the expressway's dilapidated underside was increasingly perceived as an eyesore. Meanwhile, the area near the Gardiner began to change from an industrial to an increasingly residential neighborhood.

By 2011 Toronto-based urban designer Ken Greenberg developed a new vision to repurpose the defunct elevated-highway infrastructure—imagining the areas below the expressway as an opportunity for new community spaces.

The designer recruited local supporters and in 2015 enlisted urban planner and activist Judy Matthews, who ultimately donated $32 million dollars (US$25 million) for the construction of a new public space below the Gardiner Expressway. The team brought in landscape-design firm Public Work to flesh out the idea, presented initial concepts to local officials, and received the enthusiastic endorsement of City Hall. In 2016, the Under Gardiner project then sought to establish an official name via a public competition, allowing community members, local artists, and policy experts to determine the final name: the "Bentway." Drawing inspiration from the bents, the rigid frame supports beneath the Gardiner Expressway, the project was thus armed with a grassroots-driven brand for a new public space.

The Bentway takes full advantage of its unique characteristics below the expressway. At a height of 48 feet (14.6 meters) and a width of 80 feet (24 meters), the structure creates a 1.1 mile (1.77 kilometer) curvilinear, covered trailway near historic Fort York. Following the original shoreline of Lake Ontario, the project spans across seven neighborhoods in the city, offering

dozens of separate "rooms" off the trail, which host a variety of events, activities, and programs for the community, and that connect to other outdoor spaces in the city. The addition of gardens, art exhibits and installations, performing arts spaces, fitness areas, dog parks, playgrounds, a skate trail, and farmers' markets brings new vitality along its route. A nonprofit organization, the Conservancy, maintains, operates, and leads the programs for the Bentway, with a goal of evolving its programming over time, along with the emerging interests of local communities.

The first phase of construction was completed and opened in January 2018, connecting seven local neighborhoods with roughly seventy thousand residents overall and serving as a network to the rest of the city of Toronto. The physical inverse of the highly popular High Line in New York City, the Bentway offers a compelling new public space paradigm by assigning new value to the areas below disused elevated infrastructure.

△ The expressway included both elevated and at-grade sections of road. Its location acted as a barrier between the city and Lake Ontario.

▽ The Bentway has become an opportunity to reuse the expressway, connecting the city to the waterfront and creating a new cultural attraction.

△ Stretching between Strachan Avenue and Bathurst Streets, the first phase transforms 1 mile (1.75 kilometers) of the expressway.

▽ Beneath the former expressway, the Bentway creates places for diverse programs, such as art exhibitions, gardens, and a skate trail.

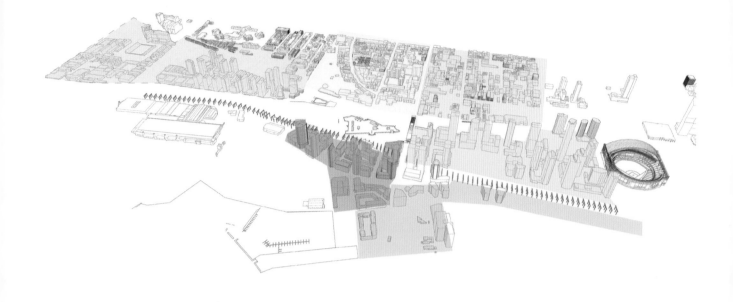

△ The initial phase of the Bentway knits together seven local neighborhoods, giving amenity to many thousands of residents.

◁ A public art program is an integral part of the Bentway, reclaiming the space for community use throughout the year.

∆ Once a primary route for cars, the expressway now provides a new artery for cyclists and pedestrians.

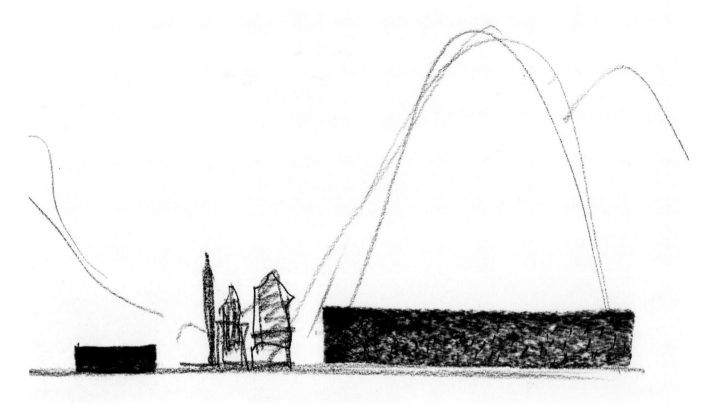

Sugar Mill
Guangxi, China
Completed 1960s
Abandoned 2002

Alila Yangshuo Hotel
Vector Architects
Transformed 2017

Δ A schematic sketch by Vector Architects expresses the relationship between the new buildings, the mill, and the karst landscape.

▷ Set in a mountainous region of southern China, the sugar mill was used for nearly eighty years before falling into disuse.

Building upon an initial structure established in the early 1920s in Yangshuo County, in the mountainous Guangxi region of southern China, a sugar mill was built in in a scenic valley in the 1960s. Surrounded by rugged, karst topography known for its hills, caves, and tunnels of limestone, the site contained several brick buildings and a trussed structure for the transport of sugarcane via the Li River. Due to the instability of sugar production in China, a succession of economic downturns, and an effort to preserve the natural environment, the mill was abandoned by 2002.

Given the extraordinary natural beauty of its location and the charm of the architectural structures, the international Alila hotel chain acquired the site and reimagined its transformation into a luxury hotel. To convert the 170,000 square foot (16,000 square meter) site, Beijing-based Vector Architects led the redesign of the structures, while Ju Bin of Horizontal Space Design repurposed the interiors. The architects designed the new hotel to have a horizontal effect, allowing the verticality of the mountains to counterbalance the structures and resolving to center their designs around the former mill's historical details.

Dong Gong, the founding partner of Vector Architects, designed a machine to produce sixty thousand bespoke hollow bricks over a six-month period, using local materials and sandstone, for the construction of the hotel's exterior walls. Locally sourced, volcanic rock was also used in the terrazzo flooring, adding a subtle splash of red color to the final design. Clay from surrounding areas was used to decorate bathrooms and headboards. The team also drew inspiration from the historical use of caves and bamboo scaffolding in the region, incorporating both elements into the site transformation.

The redesigned hotel, known as the Alila Yangshuo, is composed of 117 guest rooms. The original mill, storage buildings, and loading dock were repurposed for hotel amenities. A larger building, the Sugar House Retreat, offers private rooms overlooking mountain vistas. The Garden Townhouse faces older buildings and water features, with suites opening onto bamboo gardens or private terraces. The space between the buildings was repurposed as an open garden, featuring a sunken plaza and a reflecting pool. Walkways connect three spaces

designed to evoke the experience of caves, a reference to the natural caverns in the surrounding mountains. The 1969 Bar, built in the original sugar-pressing room, offers eighty kinds of rum and drinks focused on the theme of sugar. The sugarcane-loading dock was transformed into a swimming pool, which reflects brilliantly against the backdrop of the Li River.

Opening in the summer of 2017, the Alila Yangshuo soon became one of China's most anticipated new, high-end tourist destinations, attracting nature lovers and design enthusiasts eager to experience an elegant interplay of architecture, history, and nature. The resort has become an ethereal retreat, blending the use of local materials and crafting techniques with a seamless reverence for the rustic mountains and river on its doorstep.

漓江之滨。 蒙 紫摄影

编辑出版者：解放军画报社 社 址：北京三里河路50号 印刷者：一二零一工厂 发行者：北京市邮局 订购处：全国各地邮局(所) 总第296期 1972年第1期
电话：89·2616 电报挂号：7384 本刊代号：2——2 4 6 定价：每册一元

83

◁ Facing the waterfront, the redesigned site includes 117 guest rooms, water features, gardens, and walkways.

▽ The resort's new additions of gabled masonry structures complement the scale and form of the original industrial architecture.

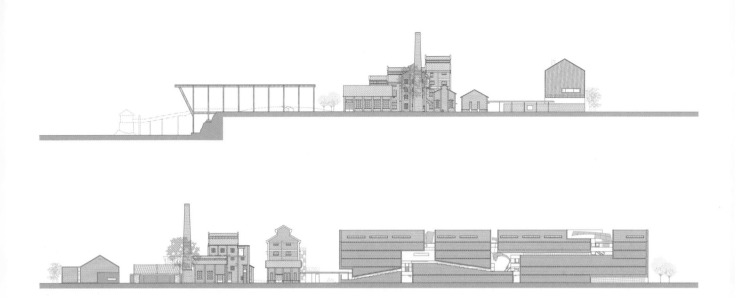

◁ Set around a central plaza and reflecting pool, the original sugar mill structures now house a reception, café, bar, gallery and multipurpose hall.

▷ The complex nestles luxurious amenities amid the dramatic topography of the region, mixing original structures with modern details.

▽ A swimming pool is inserted into an original concrete truss, formerly used to load sugar cane onto boats.

▷ Overleaf: Two new blocks containing accommodation have a deliberately simple profile and material palette—a foil to the original mill.

Dominican Church
Maastricht, Netherlands
Order of the Preachers
Completed 1294
Abandoned 1794

Boekhandel Selexyz
Dominicanen
Merkx + Girod Architects
Transformed 2005

Δ   This thirteenth-century church in the Dutch city of Maastricht had been largely abandoned since the Napoleonic invasion.

In 1294 a church was ordered by Saint Dominic and assembled by the Order of the Preachers in the Dutch city of Maastricht. The Gothic church's exterior was constructed with coal sandstone, marl, and Namur stone, and its ornate interior displayed elaborate stonework and an elegant central nave with cross rib vaults. It functioned as a religious center for centuries, despite suffering looting and partial destruction by German mercenaries in 1577. Subsequently restored, the church was utilized as a storage facility for equipment and personnel during Napoleon Bonaparte's invasion of the Netherlands in 1794. It was abandoned, and remained unchanged for nearly two centuries. At various times, it was a warehouse; a printing house; an archive; a school; a flower-exhibition center; and, until the early 2000s, perhaps the world's most elaborate and historical bicycle shed.

Seeking a compelling new location for a bookstore, in 2005 Dutch bookseller Selexyz turned to Amsterdam–based architecture firm Merkx + Girod to repurpose the church. The firm set out to create a new kind of sanctuary—this time, for reading—while restoring, celebrating,

and paying proper reverence to the religious and historical "bones" of the building. An initial design challenge was the lack of floor space; only 8,000 square feet (745 square meters) were available, and Selexyz required 13,000 square feet (1,200 square meters) to generate a profitable enterprise. The solution was to build a three-story vertical walk-in bookcase between the church's central and lateral aisles, accessible by a series of walkways and elevators, and offering a sense of immersion in both the bookstore and the church itself. The shelving was built with black-painted steel, with stylish seating, and low, horizontal reading tables set against the Gothic stone interiors. Above the bookcase are the remains of historic ceiling paintings dating back to 1337 and 1619. Popular English and Dutch titles are located on the lower shelves, and more theological or academic titles are placed higher up, closer to these religious frescoes. Lighting is strategically dispersed throughout the space, creating an ambience of reflection and quietude.

The redesign took a number of liberties in order to generate a modern sensibility, with features that might seem somewhat blasphemous

to the pious. The choir café is anchored by a large table in the shape of a crucifix, and is enlivened by the sounds of wine glasses, cappuccino machines, and the chatter of visitors. Above the table hangs a suspended lamp, which mimics a halo lighting the table. Having completed redesign projects for art destinations such as Amsterdam's Rijksmuseum, Van Gogh Museum, and the Amsterdam outpost of the Hermitage, Merkx + Girod managed to infuse a new design language into the former church, making it seem as if the Gothic structure had almost been designed to hold a vibrant modern bookstore.

Following its opening, the Boekhandel Selexyz Dominicanen was widely celebrated and remains a popular destination. Providing a fresh answer to the question of what to do with abandoned churches, it has earned the distinction of being one of the most beautiful and imaginatively repurposed bookstores in the world.

△ A schematic sketch by Merkx + Girod illustrates the principal design move: inserting a new, three-story vertical bookcase.

▽ Space for the new bookstore was created by vertically occupying the space in between the central and lateral aisles.

▷ Overleaf: The transformation of the church into a modern bookstore offers an ethereal quality to the ancient joy of reading.

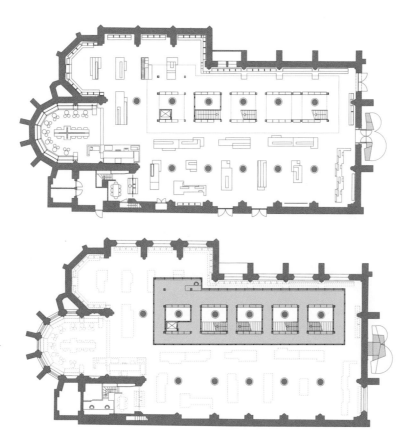

Zeche Zollverein
Essen, Germany
Haniel, Schupp and Kemmer
Completed 1847
Abandoned 1986

Zollverein Kohlenwäsche
OMA
Transformed 2007

△ The Zollverein coal mine in western Germany covered a sprawling site that became the largest of its kind in the world.

First built in the western German city of Essen by industrialist Franz Haniel, the Zollverein coal mine produced coal for over a century, from 1851 until 1986. Over time, it expanded significantly, becoming the largest coal mine in the world with an impressive array of buildings, railways, mining shafts, coking plants, and even housing and consumer amenities. In 1932 a new coal-washing facility known as Shaft 12 was opened. Designed by architects Fritz Schupp and Martin Kemmer, it immediately received attention for its Bauhaus-inspired design. Its simple, Modernist, cubical structures reflected the significance of the coal industry for the rapidly growing German nation. By the outbreak of World War II, the mine was producing 3.6 million tons of coal annually and its twin-trestle winding pit tower became a highly admired landmark within the region.

The process of coal production was modern-ized and consolidated throughout the twentieth century, resulting in the mine's owners voting for its closure in 1983. Though the 250-acre (100-hectare) plot was abandoned as an active site of coal production in 1986, the state of North Rhine-Westphalia purchased the entire complex

as a site of historical significance, worthy of preservation and repurposing. The site lay unused into the 1990s: grasses and meadows began to slowly reclaim its steel-and-brick buildings. In 2001 it was named a UNESCO World Heritage Site and local authorities focused on transforming the abandoned mine into a center of art and design, as well as a showcase of German industrial history.

In 2002 Rem Koolhaas and his team at Office for Metropolitan Architecture (OMA) were selected to redesign the former mine. Over the next eight years, OMA's master plan for redevelopment was set into motion, using the rail tracks between the coal mine and production facility to connect the various buildings to each other and to their natural surroundings. Remnant structures were transformed, becoming spaces that blended modern fixtures with the rawness of the original site and evoking its former industrial use. The Kohlenwäsche, or coal washery, was repurposed into a visitor center accessible from large outdoor escalators, illuminated with glowing orange light to remind visitors of the mine's fiery past.

Transformed into a cultural destination with an industrial-heritage museum, a design museum,

exhibition spaces, creative studios, restaurants, a theater, and even a recreational pool, Zollverein today draws over two million visitors annually. In 2007 architects Heinrich Böll and Hans Krabel worked with OMA to design the Ruhr Museum on the site of the former powerhouse, which focuses on the natural and cultural history of the Ruhr region and its coal mining history. As Germany joins other nations in attempting to decrease its production and consumption of fossil fuels, the museum takes on added significance as a key to the country's historic dependency on coal energy. Capturing the imagination of visitors several generations removed from the industrial era, Zollverein's vast grounds, rail yards, and buildings offer a valuable insight into Germany's past, and a hopeful narrative on the power of design.

△ Local authorities had a vision for the industrial building to transform into a center to showcase art, design, and Germany's industrial history.

▽ Lying unused since its closure in 1983, the site gained UNESCO World Heritage Site status almost twenty years later.

◁ The newly redesigned campus centers on an iconic twin-trestle winding pit tower.

▷ ▽ The coal washery entrance features escalators that appear to glow via a dramatic orange illumination effect, evoking the mine's legacy.

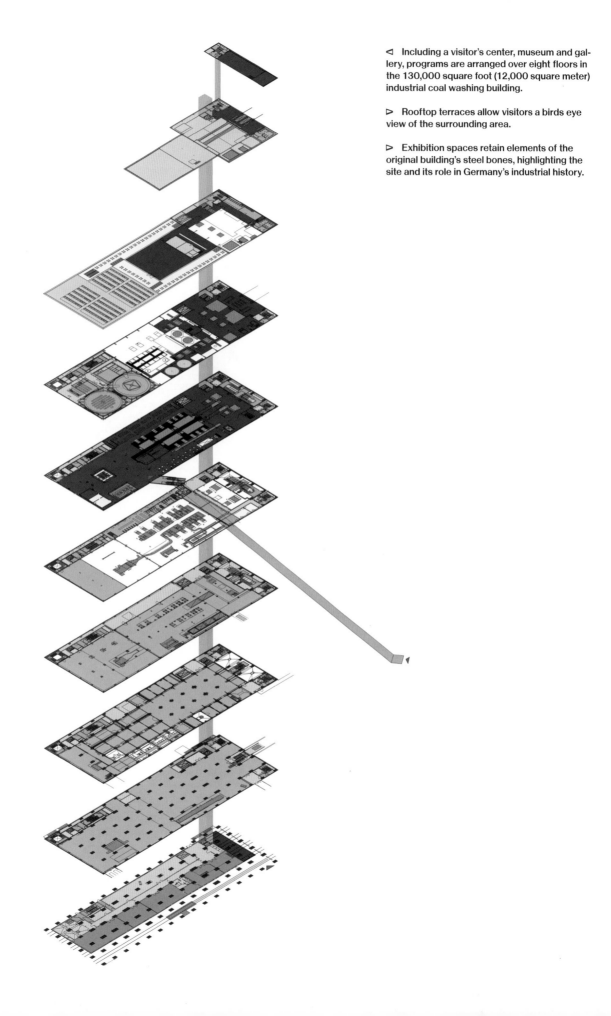

◁ Including a visitor's center, museum and gallery, programs are arranged over eight floors in the 130,000 square foot (12,000 square meter) industrial coal washing building.

▷ Rooftop terraces allow visitors a birds eye view of the surrounding area.

▷ Exhibition spaces retain elements of the original building's steel bones, highlighting the site and its role in Germany's industrial history.

**Elevated Railway
New York, NY, USA
Completed 1934
Abandoned 1980**

**High Line
James Corner Field
Operations; Diller, Scofidio
and Renfro; Piet Oudolf
Transformed 2009**

△ After 1929 elevated railway tracks on
Manhattan's West Side were built to reduce
pedestrian deaths on bustling city streets.

Amid meteoric industrial growth in the early twentieth century, New York Central Railroad freight trains carried coal, beef, and dairy products directly down Tenth and Eleventh Avenues in Manhattan. The area soon became known as "Death Avenue" due to the high degree of pedestrian accidents involving oncoming trains. To mitigate these dangers, in 1929 the West Side Improvement Project included the construction of the West Side Elevated Highway, with devoted railways overhead, separated from the city streets.

By the 1950s, interstate trucking had dramatically reduced the use of freight trains, and much of the elevated railway was demolished in the 1960s. By the 1980s, the entire viaduct had fallen into disuse, and by the 1990s it was known among locals as a rusty eyesore—particularly in the dilapidated Meatpacking District. Yet on its surface, nature reclaimed the railway, with wildflowers, weeds, grasses, and plants overtaking the abandoned trestles. With its views of the Hudson River and vantage point above the city streets, New Yorkers knew the High Line as a place of both urban decay and raw, romantic beauty.

As city officials continued to demolish elevated railways across the city, further demolition of the elevated line was halted by Chelsea resident Peter Obletz, an activist and railway enthusiast, who had challenged the efforts in court in the 1980s. In 1999 local residents Robert Hammond and Joshua David formed a not-for-profit group, Friends of the High Line, to save the structure from further demolition and to advocate for its preservation as a public park. In 2000 photographer Joel Sternfeld captured the natural beauty of the abandoned High Line, spurring local enthusiasm and support for the idea of an elevated, green space.

The administration of Mayor Michael Bloomberg saw the tremendous economic potential of a reclaimed High Line, and offered significant capital support, which Friends of the High Line leveraged to generate considerable private capital support from notable funders like Barry Diller and Diane von Furstenberg. The landscape design firm James Corner Field Operations, hired to lead the design, developed a plan to capture the wild beauty of the abandoned tracks, mixing horticultural splendor

with a surprising ambulatory experience and offering visitors surprising views while traversing multiple neighborhoods from above.

The first section of The High Line opened in 2009, with two additional sections following in 2011 and in 2014. An immediate sensation, it attracted millions of visitors in its first year and quickly led to a radical transformation of the entire neighborhood. It is today also among the world's most popular public spaces, boasting over seven million annual visitors and featuring vibrant art installations and community-oriented programming.

The global impact of the High Line extends far beyond its own popularity as a beloved and fascinating destination. It has also inspired infrastructure reclamation projects around the world, serving as the prime example of the extraordinary economic and cultural potential of new public spaces in underdeveloped neighborhoods. While generating billions of dollars in increased real estate and retail revenue, the High Line also stands as a compelling model for public-private development in public spacemaking.

△ Abandoned by the 1980s, the High Line railway tracks remained rusty ruins above an industrial neighborhood.

▽ The dilapidated tracks became consumed with weeds, plants, rubbish, and trees after decades of neglect.

▷ ▽ Designs sought to unify the elevated railway with the street level while introducing an ambitious landscape design.

◁ The revitalized High Line creates a green ribbon park extending several miles through multiple city neighborhoods.

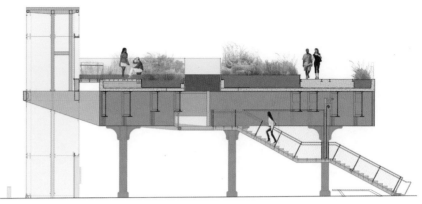

▷ Various segments of the High Line are reserved for sitting, public events, and observing the streets below.

▽ The High Line provides views of the Hudson River, lifting visitors above the dense sidewalks for a fresh perspective on the city.

◁ Significant new real estate development has emerged along the High Line's length, immersing visitors physically in a visibly growing city.

◁ The surprising juxtaposition of natural elements and former infrastructure evokes the dreamlike state of the once abandoned railway.

Coal Crane
Copenhagen, Denmark
Completed 1944
Abandoned 1990s

The Krane
Arcgency
Transformed 2017

△ A striking mid-century coal crane was built in a Copenhagen port but was left abandoned as the area fell into a postindustrial era of decline.

The Nordhavn port area of Copenhagen, an industrial zone with decades of history in the shipping industry, fell into significant decline by the end of the twentieth century. The Danish Government and the City of Copenhagen led an effort, beginning in 2005, to redevelop the entire neighborhood, overseeing a community engagement process and staging a series of international design competitions to attract innovative repurposing ideas.

Local developer Klaus Kastbjerg had already tried his hand at creative reuse of abandoned industrial infrastructure, having transformed a former grain silo in Copenhagen into a residential apartment building, and collaborated with architect Mads Møller of Argency to convert a disused crane for a meeting space. Inspired by the potential of transforming a second crane into a private oasis, Kastbjerg and Møller reunited to re-envision an abandoned coal crane at the heart of the Nordhavn district, moving it to a new location and subjecting it to two years of renovation.

Optimizing the unique characteristics of the structure itself, a new retreat was designed with multiple levels, including a reception area on the ground floor, a meeting room on the first floor, a spa and terrace on the second floor, and a multiroom living area on the top floor. A minimal approach was taken in the overall design, reflecting a typically Danish view of the meaning of luxury itself. In a nod to the structure's previous use for coal transport, the living quarters are outfitted entirely in various hues of black, and utilize natural materials such as stone, steel, wood, and leather. The design intention was to remove visual distractions—"bells and whistles"— so that guests would feel more connected to their surroundings and the external atmosphere.

Windows entirely envelop the space, allowing visitors a theatrical view of the Copenhagen harbor. In the 540 square foot (50 square meter) living space on the top floor, built-in custom furniture, from a pull-down bed to cupboards and seating areas, were crafted by hand by local artisans and designed to recede sculpturally, offering a sense of monochromatic serenity. Fifty feet (fifteen meters) above the ground, the bedroom offers panoramic views, extending beyond an industrial stretch of waterfront to as far away as the Swedish coastline. The broader Scandinavian

influence on the overall aesthetic of the space is underscored by the ability to view the bridge connecting Denmark to Sweden across the Øresund strait, and is reflected in the selection of appliance brands like Bang & Olufsen, Kvadrat, and Sweden's Carpe Diem Beds.

The space takes advantage of the specific natural environment of Copenhagen, known for longer-than-average hours of sunlight in summer and shorter days in winter. Inside the refurbished space, one feels connected to the water and surrounding weather patterns in a visceral manner. It offers a unique way in which to celebrate and showcase the rich history and industrial infrastructure of one of the last remaining harbors in the Danish capital. The Krane is a compelling lesson in the power of moody simplicity to achieve an atmosphere of relaxation and solitude.

△ As the city of Copenhagen sought to transform the surrounding neighborhood, it called for ideas to reimagine a future for the crane.

▽ Reimagined as the Krane, the new facility is a retreat set over multiple levels and includes a meeting room and accommodation at the top.

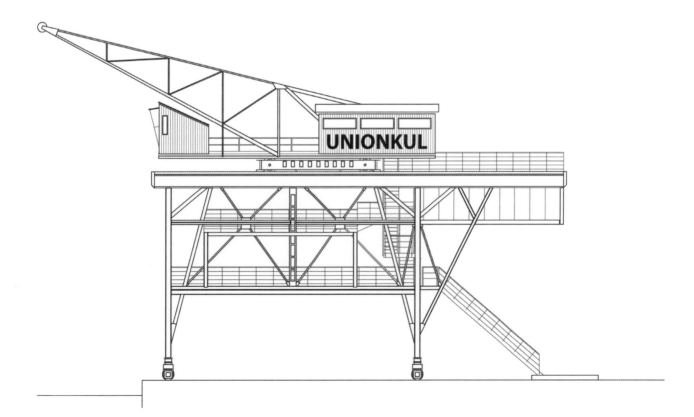

△ The Krane features a conference room with sweeping views of the harbor.

▷ The color palette and materials for the redesign evoke both the local industrial environment and Scandinavian design.

△ The design transforms the industrial structure into an oasis, with interiors designed to instill a sense of serenity and connection to nature.

▷ Overleaf: The Krane offers a unique perspective on the river, the city, and the possibilities for reclaimed industrial structures.

Stony Island Trust and Savings Bank
Chicago, IL, USA
William Gibbons Uffendell
Completed 1923
Abandoned 1980s

Stony Island Arts Bank
Theaster Gates
Transformed 2015

Δ   The Stony Island Trust building is an elegant, imposing Classical Revival design for a Chicago community bank.

On the South Side of Chicago, the Stony Island Trust and Savings Bank Building was constructed in 1923. A symbol of the growing prosperity of the neighborhood's middle- and working-class community, the bank was built in Classical Revival Style by architect William Gibbons Uffendell, featuring great fluted columns and evoking the feeling of a modern temple. The 17,000 square foot (1,580 square meter) building was designed with a two-story arcaded hall for bank tenants, with a grand, coffered, barrel-vaulted ceiling overhead. The third floor, built for rentable office space, featured elegant wood-and-glass-lined corridors and rooms.

Hobbled by the Great Depression, the bank itself was out of business by 1931. Over the next few decades, a succession of banks purchased and sold the building while major demographic and economic changes took hold in the surrounding area. By the 1970s Chicago's South Side had been transformed into a predominantly African-American community, while a lack of investment in the neighborhood led to significant deterioration and demolition of local buildings. In the 1980s, the building had been vacated, and was abandoned for nearly three decades.

In 2012 local Chicago installation artist and urbanist Theaster Gates and his nonprofit organization, the Rebuild Foundation, purchased the building for one dollar and set about transforming the space into a community amenity to house a new kind of arts organization. Building upon previous reclamation efforts known as the Dorchester Projects, in which four nearby abandoned buildings had been converted into community venues, Gates first set out to raise five hundred thousand dollars by salvaging marble slabs from the site and selling them at the Art Basel art fair as "bank bonds." With additional resources, Gates then took on the mission of transforming the space to preserve its historical integrity and envision a more robust civic purpose for it.

His redesign retained key details of the historical bank—including marble doors, plaster archways, terrazzo-tile floors, vaulted ceilings, and wooden telephone booths—while new furniture was custom built using reclaimed wood from local structures like water towers. Opening in 2015, the Stony Island Arts Bank was rehabilitated into a multipurpose space devoted to the promotion of art, architecture, and black culture. The

space features an archive of black publications like *Jet*, *Ebony*, and *Negro Digest*, alongside a small collection of racist collectibles known as "negrobilia," which a prominent African-American banker acquired in order to remove offensive materials from public circulation. A wood-paneled room contains a collection of vinyl records from the "godfather of house music," DJ Frankie Knuckles, and the building also features sixty thousand antique glass lantern slides of historical art and architectural images. A reading room and rotating set of community-focused installations ensure a vibrant hum to the space, which has been designed to serve as a hub for art enthusiasts and local residents alike.

In reclaiming the former financial center as a new cultural center, Gates infused this transformation with a sense of social and racial justice. The Stony Island Arts Bank boldly addresses a legacy of racial discrimination in Chicago and across the United States, with an emphasis on underrepresented narratives on African-American culture, history, and heritage.

△ A potent symbol of Chicago's prosperity, the bank and surrounding neighborhood fell into decline after the Great Depression.

▽ The building was utterly abandoned and by the 1980s was in a state of severe dilapidation.

Δ ◁ Though abandoned, the details of remnants testified to the bank's grand interior details, from ornate ceilings to intricate vaults.

▷ The redesigned and refurbished building reveals both a polished claim to its former glory and a hard earned patina.

▷ Overleaf: Now a multipurpose facility celebrating art, architecture, black culture, and the surrounding community, the grand library includes vital African-American archives.

Gasholders
London, England
Completed 1860–67
Abandoned 2001

Gasholders London
Wilkinson Eyre
Transformed 2017

△ Massive cylinders to hold two million cubic feet of gas were built in London's King's Cross neighborhood in the late-nineteenth century.

Built and refurbished between 1860 and 1880, three interlocking gasholders arose in London's King's Cross neighborhood to store the gas demanded by a rapidly growing city. Massive, imposing cylinders, each held 2 million cubic feet (over 55,000 cubic meters) of gas, enough to supply 2,400 homes daily. It was the largest gasworks in the world, in a strategic central location adjacent to key railways and a canal. The gasholders were framed with three tiers of hollow, cylindrical columns along with riveted, wrought iron lattice girders. As energy-storage technology evolved, and North Sea gas was discovered in the 1960s, the King's Cross structures became increasingly less critical until their eventual decommission. After nearby St. Pancras railway station was expanded in the 1990s, the structures were, by 2001, left abandoned.

Meanwhile, real estate developer Argent had, since 2000, begun a massive redevelopment of the entire King's Cross neighborhood, investing US$4 billion (£3 billion) to transform sixty-seven acres (twenty-seven hectares) of former railway lands. The master plan engaged dozens of architects to reimagine a broad array of former

industrial buildings, in one of the largest such redevelopments in Europe. In 2002, London-based architectural firm Wilkinson Eyre was selected to repurpose the steel frames of the three gasholders into a new luxury residential project. The Grade II-listed frames were carefully dismantled with twenty-ton cranes, and transported to the Yorkshire workshop of Shepley Engineers, a highly skilled team that had previously supported the renovation of St. Pancras station roof.

The structures were returned to the site after refurbishment, and construction on the new residential towers began in 2014. The designs took full advantage of the circular spaces, arranging glass-walled dwellings along the perimeters, using the original cast iron as frames, and installing skylights at the core of each building, in order to fill each central atrium with natural light. To allow for larger or smaller "wedges" for apartments of different sizes, the 145 residences were carved out of each building like slices of pie. The radial walls of each apartment were outfitted with mirrors, to give the perception of a continuous, circular space. Large private balconies or terraces were positioned to give stunning

views of the city and waterfront. Perforated steel screens, which can be opened or closed for privacy and protection from the sun, add a luxurious yet industrial feel to each apartment. Amenities like rooftop gardens, gyms, spas, workspaces, and event spaces provide additional touches of luxury. Between the three gasholders is a pool of water, representing the very point that the three structures meet.

The new Gasholder London residential buildings, which opened in 2018, became instantly recognizable icons within a radically transformed neighborhood. Adjacent to the site, a fourth gasholder was repurposed into a public, green space known as Gasholder Park. The redevelopment displays an inspired use of a quirky cylindrical shape and a challenging preservation design. But it is not the last of its kind; a similar project is being undertaken in Stockholm and, in 2017, the Royal Institute of British Architects ran an ideas competition to foster ideas for the repurposing of decommissioned gasholder sites across the UK.

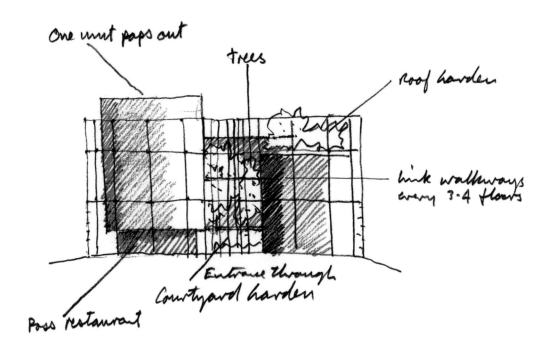

One unit pops out

trees

roof garden

link walkways every 3-4 floors

Entrance through Courtyard garden

Pass Restaurant

△ This schematic sketch imagines the gasholder in its new use as luxury residential accommodation set around a courtyard garden.

▽ By the turn of the millennium, the grand gasholders had been decommissioned and were eventually abandoned.

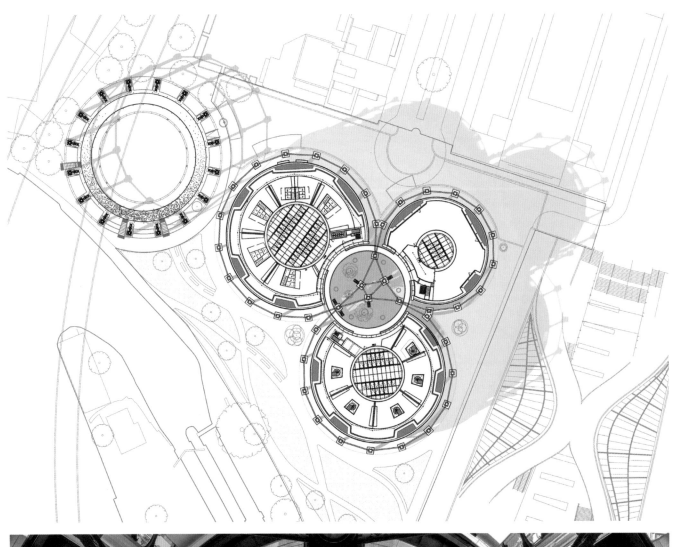

△ Occupying the northwest edge of the King's Cross redevelopment, the gasholders lie adjacent to the Regent's Canal.

▷ The new use of the Grade-II listed, cast iron gasholders maintains the original and distinctive lattice, with steel-and-glass cladding set behind this framework.

◁ To introduce light and air into each of the three redeveloped gasholders, the apartments are set around central courtyards with dedicated atria and cores.

Δ A dramatic skylit atrium is the main focus of
the lobby of each apartment block. Vertical white
timber panels emphasise the building's height.

▷ Drawing on the existing circular plan, apartments are arranged in segments with central
circulation, and living/bedrooms at the periphery.

Laverstoke Mill
Hampshire, England
Completed 1724
Abandoned 2005

Bombay Sapphire Distillery
Heatherwick Studio
Transformed 2014

△ A series of brick buildings in Laverstoke were built for one of the most prominent paper mills in the country, but abandoned by 2005.

Laverstoke Mill, situated in the bucolic Hampshire countryside west of London, was originally used for grinding corn as early as 1086. In 1724, the facility was transformed to exclusively produce banknote paper for the recently established Bank of England. The site of five royal visits during its tenure as a paper mill, in 1860 it also began producing the paper for British-Indian rupees. The complex, sitting atop the River Test and growing over time to include over forty buildings, continued in business until 1963, when papermaking at Laverstoke Mill ceased. Despite various plans to reuse the site, the paper mill was eventually left vacant by 2005, with its historic buildings entirely abandoned.

Seeking an iconic home, gin company Bombay Sapphire purchased the five-acre (two-hectare) site, and in 2010 commissioned Heatherwick Studio to renovate and convert the former mill into a public-facing gin distillery. Thomas Heatherwick's design team was challenged to reimagine the potential of the complex after its disjointed growth over several centuries. Its numerous structures sprawled across the original mill site, with multiple architectural styles and

varied connectivity between them. The river running through the complex, formerly popular with fly fishermen, had been narrowed and partially hidden in an unsightly concrete channel.

Heatherwick's team first removed the twenty most recently erected structures, while restoring the remaining twenty-three historic Georgian and Victorian brick and stone buildings. The site was unified by widening the River Test, celebrating the river with the cultivation of fresh wildflowers and grasses, and running it through the middle of a new, central courtyard. Two intertwining greenhouses in sweeping metal frames that spread out like futuristic spider webs were built to house the tropical and temperate botanicals used as ingredients for the gin. Due to different survival requirements, tropical plants are cultivated in one of the greenhouses, while Mediterranean specimens are kept in the other; together, they house the ten species used in the production of the gin. These striking new structures flow gracefully out of the historic buildings, like cocktails being poured, and offer bold, science-oriented, experiential windows into both the production process and the complex itself.

A variety of innovative features earned the distillery refurbishment an "Outstanding" rating under BREEAM (the UK Building Research Establishment's Environmental Assessment Method) for environmental sustainability—the first time that a refurbished structure had earned this accolade. The necessarily warm temperature within the greenhouses is maintained with the excess heat generated during the distillation process, which would otherwise be discarded. In addition to photovoltaic power systems, a preexisting turbine was restored to be used in tandem with an electricity-generating system. Byproducts of the botanical production process are reused as fuel in a biomass boiler, harvested rainwater is used throughout the site, and key building materials included reused and recycled bricks and roofing tiles.

Completed in 2014, the Bombay Sapphire Distillery is today open to visitors, who can tour the newly refurbished structures; learn about the production process within the facility and its botanical greenhouses; attend cocktail mixology classes; and, of course, enjoy that classic British drink, the gin and tonic.

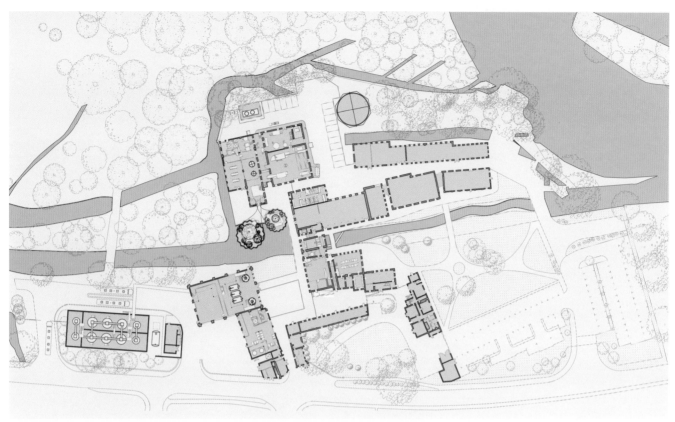

△ The masterplan for the new development stripped away more recent bulldings, retaining and restoring the original Georgian structures.

▽ The revitalized compound includes rehabil- itated historic buildings of brick alongside new, modern insertions of glass.

△ Bombay's new defining feature is the installation of two adjacent greenhouses, one for Mediterranean plants, the other for tropical.

◁ ▷ Visitor tours of the facility reveal the full extent of gin distillation onsite, including its ingredients, processing, and manufacture.

▷ Together, the greenhouses propagate the ten botanicals used in Bombay Sapphire's gin. Plants are sustained by excess heat created through the distillation process.

△ With a whimsical design that evokes a gin
cocktail being poured, the two greenhouses offer
an all-season connection to the natural world.

Index

Picture Credits

Every reasonable attempt has been made to identify owners of copyright. Errors and omissions notified to the publisher will be corrected in subsequent editions. T – top, B – bottom.

123RF 49T; STF/AFP 18T; Mark Dyball/ Alamy Stock Photo 221B; Keystone Pictures USA/Alamy Stock Photo 29B; James D Evans - Architectural Photography/Alamy Stock Photo 36B; Alamy Stock Photo 56B; Photography by Roos Aldershoff 190TR; Images courtesy of Arcgency 208-213; Archivo General de la Nación (AGN), Archivo Histórico Fundidora (AHF), Parque Fundidora y Fototeca, N.L. 130; Avanti Architects 75B, 101-103; Iwan Baan 59T, 59B, 110-111, 112, 113, 114, 115, 204, 205B, 206-207; David Baker 31B; Images courtesy of The Bentway Conservancy 177B-181; Darren Bradley 42B; Jon Bruner 21B; Collection of The Buffalo History Museum 26B; Caters News Agency 20T, 20B; Roberto Conte 62T/B; DANA Arquitectos 84-87; depositphotos 54B; Courtesy of the Burton Historical Collection, Detroit Public Library 49B; Permissions courtesy Dion Neutra, Architect and Richard and Dion Neutra Papers, Department of Special Collections, Charles E. Young Research Library, UCLA 16T, 16B; DLANDstudio and WXY, courtesy of The Trust for Public Land 88-91; Courtesy of Dorte Mandrup Arkitekter 68-71; Andrew Einhorn 83T; ERZ Limited 74B; Georges Fessy 165B, 168; Roberto Marossi / Courtesy of Fondazione Prada 142; Photograph by Bas Princen, Courtesy of Fondazione Prada 145B, 146-147; Fred Morley/Fox Photos/Getty Images 60T; Trevor Freeman 27T, 27B; Keystone-France/ GAMMA RAPHO 18B; Giancarlo Botti/GAMMA RAPHO 19; Geo. P. Hall & Son/The New York Historical Society/Getty Images 22B, 32T; China Photos/Getty Images 100T, 101T; Fox Photos/Hulton Archive/Getty Images 150T; Richard Baker / In Pictures via Getty Images 151T; View Pictures/UIG via Getty Images 152, 154; In Pictures Ltd./Corbis via Getty Images 155B; Will Wintercross/Bloomberg via Getty Images 155T; Hulton Archive/Getty Images 21T; Walter Leporati/Getty Images 22T; Authenticated News/Getty Images 29T; Stephen Bardens/Getty Images 30B; Paul Kaye; Cordaiy Photo Library Ltd./CORBIS/Corbis via Getty Images 30T; Al Fenn/The LIFE Images Collection/Getty Images 32B; Bettmann/Getty Images 33, 37B; English Heritage/Heritage Images/Getty Images 35T; Jim Dyson/Getty Images 36T; Lee Balterman/The LIFE Images Collection/ Getty Images 37T; Geography Photos/UIG via Getty Images 45B; DIMITAR DILKOFF/AFP/ Getty Images 45T; PHILIPPE DESMAZES/ AFP/Getty Images 46T; Feng Li/Getty Images 47T; Sean Gallup/Getty Images 52B; William Vandivert/The LIFE Picture Collection/Getty Images 52T; Martin Sachse/ullstein bild via Getty Images 53B; Ralf Gebhardt/ullstein bild via Getty Images 53T; Yasuo Tomishige/The Asahi Shimbun via Getty Images 54T; JOSE JORDAN/ AFP/Getty Images 55B; Ioanna Sakellaraki /

Barcroft Im / Barcroft Media via Getty Images 57B; Tony Triolo /ABC via Getty Images 57T; © CORBIS/Corbis via Getty Images 58T; David McNew/Getty Images 77T; © Jeff Goldberg / Esto 17T; With permission by Ryan Gravel , 92T 93T; Grimshaw architects 131; Maria Gruzdeva 63T; Steve Hall 217, 218-219; © Rob 'tHart 118, 119, 120, 121; Hilton Teper / Heatherwick Studio 108; Heatherwick Studio 109, 226-231; © Herzog & de Meuron 152; Photography: Ariel Huber, Lausanne 24T, 25; sJohn W. Iwanski/ Flickr 34B; JAKOB + MACFARLANE 136-141; James Johnson 75T; Kalmbach Publishing Co 202; Thorsten Klapsch 28B; Simon Cockerell / Koryo Tours 47B; Peter Lander 222B, 223, 224-225; Diana Larrea 43; Courtesy of Lela Goren Group 50B, 51; Library of Congress 76T; Lowline 81T, 83B; © John Maclean/VIEW 151T; Mary Evans 56T; Historic England / Mary Evans 220; Masterfile 44T; Thomas Mayer 197T, 199, 201T; McGinlay Bell Architects Ltd 73B, 74T, 75T; Photo: Roos Aldershoff / Merkx+Girod / Merk X architects and designers 192-195; Merkx+Girod / Merk X architects and designers 190TL, 191; Arwed Messmer 28T; © 2018. Image copyright TheMetropolitan Museum of Art/Art Resource/ Scala, Florence 26T; Museum of Innovation and Science 50T; © MVRDV 117; New York Post 203T; New York Transit Museum 80; Ateliers Jean Nouvel 166; NYC Municipal Archives 203B; Image courtesy OMA 143, 144; OMA 145T; Photograph by Iwan Baan, Courtesy of OMA 148-149; Philippe Ruault / OMA 196, 197B; Photos by Anselm van Sintfiet / OMA 198, 201B; OMA 200; Courtesy of OMA and OLIN 96-99; Perkins + Will / ABI 94T; Perkins + Will / Flyworx 94B; Perkins+Will / Ralph Daniel 93B, 95B; Courtesy of Perkins+Will 78T, 79T, 79B; Photo courtesy of PhillyHistory. org, a project of the Philadelphia Department of Records 48T; Photograph by Madan Mahatta / Courtesy PHOTOINK 24B; Piuarch 122-123, 124; Photo: Andrea Martiradonna / Piuarch 124B, 125B, 127, 128-129; Photo: Helene Binet / Piuarch 124T; Photo: Giovanni Hanninen / Piuarch 125T; Photo: Sara Pooley 214, 215B, 216TB; Raad Studio 81B, 82; Charles Ragucci 48B; REUTERS News Agency 116; Photo: Jon-Marc Creaney / RIBA Collections 72T; RIBA Collections 73T; RICARDO BOFILL TALLER DE ARQUITECTURA 156-163; Paul Rivera 132-133, 134-135; Philippe Ruault 167, 169; Photo: Richard Nickel / Richard Nickel Archive, Ryerson & Burnham Archives, The Art Institute of Chicago. Digital File # 201006_180628-001/201006_110815-042 23B; Shutterstock 46B; Photomarine / Shutterstock.com 55T; Photo: Margherita Spiluttini / Architekturzentrum Wien, Collection 58B, 153, 164, 165T; Albino Tavares 60B, 61; Tetra Tech, Inc 78B; City of Toronto Archive Photos 176, 177T; Valdis Zusmanis 95T; Reginald Van de Velde 44B; Annemie Vanwetswinkel 31T; Images courtesy of Vector Architects 182-189; Aurelien Villette 63B; Wenink \ Holtkamp Architecten 170-175; Wikipedia 23T, 35B; Wilkinson Eyre 221T, 222T; World Monuments Fund 17B, 42T

Acknowledgments

The author wishes to acknowledge some of the many individuals who shaped the idea and the execution of this book. Without Keith Fox's vision and encouragement, this entire project would never have begun, and I am deeply thankful for his faith in me and in the concept. Virginia McLeod, part-commissioning editor, part-encouraging coach, was a delight to work with as she transformed the idea into a clearer shape for an actual book. I was highly fortunate to collaborate with the experienced and resourceful editors Rebecca Roke and Sarah Bell throughout the writing, editing, and image procurement. Jake Gianaris and Luke Polihrom, my research assistants, helped uncover valuable research on hundreds of potential projects, and drafted initial texts for final selections. A debt of gratitude must go to all the project leaders and design teams who took time to help procure images and materials, but I must go a step further and thank them personally for their inspiring work, that continues to shape the exciting global direction in re-designing abandoned spaces. I would like to thank my friend and fellow cofounder of the Lowline, James Ramsey, for sharing his brilliant idea with me and for allowing me to tag along on the most adventurous professional journey of my life. Most of all, this effort would never have been possible without the persistent encouragement and support of Robert Hammond, who is my constant source of inspiration and love, a relentless font of optimism and creativity, and the one who has taught me the most about pursuing audacious dreams without fear.

Phaidon Press Ltd.
Regent's Wharf
All Saint's Street
London N1 9PA

Phaidon Press Inc.
65 Bleecker Street
New York, NY 10012

phaidon.com

First published 2019
© 2019 Phaidon Press Limited
ISBN 978 0 7148 7802 7

A CIP catalogue record of this book is available
from the British Library and the Library of
Congress.

All rights reserved.
No part of this publication may be reproduced,
stored in a retrieval system or transmitted in any
form or by any means, electronic, mechanical,
photocopying, recording or otherwise, without
the written permission of Phaidon Press Ltd.

Commissioning Editor
Virginia McLeod

Project Editor
Rebecca Roke

Picture Editor
Sarah Bell

Production Controller
Sarah Kramer

Design
Neil Donnelly

Typesetting
Albino Tavares

Printed in China